CATHOLIC TREASURY
of
PRAYERS

All honor and glory to our Lord and our God.

CATHOLIC TREASURY of PRAYERS

A COLLECTION OF PRAYERS
FOR ALL TIMES AND SEASONS

Illustrated

CATHOLIC BOOK PUBLISHING CORP.
New Jersey

NIHIL OBSTAT: Sr. M. Kathleen Flanagan, S.C., Ph.D.
Censor Librorum

IMPRIMATUR: ✠ Frank J. Rodimer, J.C.D.
Bishop of Paterson

The Nihil Obstat and Imprimatur are official declarations that a book or pamphlet is free of doctrinal or moral error. No implication is contained therein that those who have granted the Nihil Obstat and Imprimatur agree with the contents, opinions or statements expressed.

ABBREVIATIONS OF THE BOOKS OF THE BIBLE

Acts—Acts of the Apostles
Am—Amos
Bar—Baruch
1 Chr—1 Chronicles
2 Chr—2 Chronicles
Col—Colossians
1 Cor—1 Corinthians
2 Cor—2 Corinthians
Dn—Daniel
Dt—Deuteronomy
Eccl—Ecclesiastes
Eph—Ephesians
Est—Esther
Ex—Exodus
Ez—Ezekiel
Ezr—Ezra
Gal—Galatians
Gn—Genesis
Hb—Habakkuk
Heb—Hebrews
Hg—Haggai
Hos—Hosea
Is—Isaiah
Jas—James
Jb—Job
Jdt—Judith
Jer—Jeremiah
Jgs—Judges
Jl—Joel
Jn—John
1 Jn—1 John
2 Jn—2 John
3 Jn—3 John
Jon—Jonah
Jos—Joshua
Jude—Jude
1 Kgs—1 Kings
2 Kgs—2 Kings
Lam—Lamentations
Lk—Luke
Lv—Leviticus
Mal—Malachi
1 Mc—1 Maccabees
2 Mc—2 Maccabees
Mi—Micah
Mk—Mark
Mt—Matthew
Na—Nahum
Neh—Nehemiah
Nm—Numbers
Ob—Obadiah
Phil—Philippians
Phlm—Philemon
Prv—Proverbs
Ps(s)—Psalms
1 Pt—1 Peter
2 Pt—2 Peter
Rom—Romans
Ru—Ruth
Rv—Revelation
Sir—Sirach
1 Sm—1 Samuel
2 Sm—2 Samuel
Song—Song of Songs
Tb—Tobit
1 Thes—1 Thessalonians
2 Thes—2 Thessalonians
Ti—Titus
1 Tm—1 Timothy
2 Tm—2 Timothy
Wis—Wisdom
Zec—Zechariah
Zep—Zephaniah

(T-938)

Printed in China 24 HA 2
catholicbookpublishing.com

INTRODUCTION

THIS treasury is a prayer companion for all time. It will accompany you on your prayer journey during different times of the day, different days of the week, different months of the year, and different liturgical seasons.

You can turn to this prayerbook while you worship at Sunday or daily Mass, the Church's greatest prayer. An entire section is devoted to prayers that can be said before and after Communion.

This prayerbook will provide food for contemplation during visits to the Blessed Sacrament or as you meditate on the sufferings and death of Jesus while praying the Stations of the Cross.

There also are a number of familiar and perhaps not-so-familiar Psalms included in this treasury. These universal prayers, the public prayer par excellence of the People of God, will offer you the opportunity to recall the truths that God revealed to the Chosen People as well as experience the gamut of human emotions that the Psalms encompass.

This prayerbook features sections devoted to prayers to Our Blessed Mother, St. Joseph, and Patron Saints. These prayers can serve as the basis of the words you speak to those who intercede with God on your behalf.

This collection of prayers is a worthy accompaniment to the Christian life. It also serves as a reminder of the words of St. John Chrysostom, Doctor of the Church, who said: "It is possible to offer fervent prayer even while walking in public or strolling alone, or seated in your shop, . . . while buying or selling, . . . or even while cooking."

May this treasury help you to believe fervently in these profound words of St. John Chrysostom: "Nothing is equal to prayer; for what is impossible, it makes possible, what is difficult, easy."

CONTENTS

Jesus urged us to pray daily.

POPULAR PRAYERS

The Sign of the Cross

IN the name of the Father, and of the Son, ✠ and of the Holy Spirit. Amen.

The Lord's Prayer

OUR Father, Who art in heaven, hallowed be Thy name; Thy kingdom come, Thy will be done on earth as it is in heaven. Give us this day our daily bread, and forgive us our trespasses, as we forgive those who trespass against us; and lead us not into temptation, but deliver us from evil. Amen.

The Hail Mary

HAIL, Mary, full of grace! The Lord is with thee; blessed art thou among women, and blessed is the fruit of thy womb, Jesus. Holy Mary, Mother of God, pray for us sinners now and at the hour of our death. Amen.

Glory Be to the Father

GLORY be to the Father, and to the Son, and to the Holy Spirit. As it was in the beginning, is now, and ever shall be. Amen.

The Apostles' Creed

I BELIEVE in God, the Father almighty, Creator of heaven and earth, and in Jesus Christ, His only Son, Our Lord, Who was conceived by the Holy Spirit, born of the Virgin Mary, suffered under Pontius Pilate, was crucified, died and was buried; He descended into hell; on the third day He rose again from the dead; He ascended into heaven, and is seated at the right hand of God the Father almighty; from there He will come to judge the living and the dead.

I believe in the Holy Spirit, the holy catholic Church, the communion of Saints, the forgiveness of sins, the resurrection of the body, and life everlasting. Amen.

An Act of Faith

O MY God, I firmly believe that You are one God in three Divine Persons, Father, Son, and Holy Spirit. I believe that Your Divine Son became Man, and died for our sins, and He will come to judge the living and the dead.

I believe these and all the truths that the Holy Catholic Church teaches because You have revealed them, Who can neither deceive nor be deceived. Amen.

An Act of Hope

O MY God, relying on Your almighty power and infinite mercy and promises, I hope to obtain pardon for my sins, the help of Your grace, and life everlasting, through the merits of Jesus Christ, my Lord and Redeemer. Amen.

An Act of Love

O MY God, I love You above all things, with my whole heart and soul, because You are all-good and worthy of all love.

I love my neighbor as myself for the love of You. I forgive all who have injured me, and ask pardon of all whom I have injured. Amen.

An Act of Contrition

O MY God, I am heartily sorry for having offended You, and I detest all my sins because of Your just punishments, but most of all because they offend You, my God, Who are all-good and deserving of all my love. I firmly resolve, with the help of Your grace, to sin no more and to avoid the unnecessary occasions of sin. Amen.

Prayer to the Holy Spirit

COME, Holy Spirit, fill the hearts of Your faithful and kindle in them the fire of Your love.

℣. Send forth Your Spirit, and they shall be created.

℟. And You shall renew the face of the earth.

Let us pray. O God, You instructed the hearts of the faithful by the light of the Holy Spirit. Grant that, by the gift of the same Spirit, we may be always truly wise, and ever rejoice in His consolation. Through Christ our Lord. Amen.

The Angelus

℣. The Angel of the Lord declared unto Mary.

℟. And she conceived of the Holy Spirit.
Hail Mary, etc.

℣. Behold the handmaid of the Lord.

℟. Be it done unto me according to your word.
Hail Mary, etc.

℣. And the Word was made flesh.

℟. And dwelt among us.
Hail Mary, etc.

℣. Pray for us, O holy Mother of God.

℟. That we may be made worthy of the promises of Christ.

Let us pray. Pour forth, we beseech You, O Lord, Your grace into our hearts, that we to whom the Incarnation of Christ, Your Son, was made known by the message of an Angel, may by His Passion and Cross be brought to the glory of His Resurrection, through the same Christ our Lord. Amen.

Regina Caeli

(said during Eastertide instead of The Angelus)

QUEEN of heaven, rejoice, alleluia.
For He Whom you merited to bear, alleluia.
Has risen as He said, alleluia.
Pray for us to God, alleluia.

℣. Rejoice and be glad, O Virgin Mary, alleluia.

℟. Because the Lord is truly risen, alleluia.

Let us pray. O God, by the Resurrection of Your Son, our Lord Jesus Christ, You granted joy to the whole world. Grant, we beg You, that, through the intercession of the Virgin Mary, His Mother, we may attain the joys of eternal life. Through the same Christ our Lord. Amen.

Hail, Holy Queen

HAIL, Holy Queen, Mother of mercy, hail, our life, our sweetness, and our hope! To you do we cry, poor banished children of Eve! To you do we send up our sighs, mourning, and weeping in this vale of tears!

Turn then, most gracious advocate, your eyes of mercy toward us; and after this, our exile, show unto us the blessed fruit of your womb, Jesus! O clement, O loving, O sweet Virgin Mary!

Blessing before Meals

BLESS us, O Lord, and these Your gifts, which we are about to receive from Your bounty, through Christ our Lord. Amen.

Grace after Meals

WE give You thanks for all Your benefits, O Almighty God, Who live and reign forever. Amen.

May the souls of the faithful departed, through the mercy of God, rest in peace. Amen.

DAILY PRAYERS

MORNING PRAYERS

Offering to the Holy Trinity

MOST holy and adorable Trinity, one God in three Persons, I praise You and give You thanks for all the favors You have bestowed upon me. Your goodness has preserved me until now. I offer You my whole being and in particular all my thoughts, words and deeds, together with all the trials I may undergo this day. Give them Your blessing. May Your Divine Love animate them and may they serve Your greater glory.

I make this morning offering in union with the Divine intentions of Jesus Christ Who offers himself daily in the holy Sacrifice of the Mass, and in union with Mary, His Virgin Mother and our Mother, who was always the faithful handmaid of the Lord.

Glory be to the Father, and to the Son, and to the Holy Spirit. Amen.

For Divine Guidance through the Day

LORD, God Almighty, You have brought us safely to the beginning of this day. Defend us today by Your mighty power, that we may not fall into any sin, but that all our words may so proceed and all our thoughts and actions be so directed, as to be always just in your sight. Through Christ our Lord. Amen.

Direct, we beg You, O Lord, our actions by Your holy inspirations, and carry them on by Your gracious assistance, that every prayer and work of ours may begin always with You, and through You be happily ended. Amen.

Morning Offering

O MY God, I offer You all my prayers, works, and sufferings, in union with the Sacred Heart of Jesus, for the intentions for which He pleads and offers Himself in the Holy Sacrifice of the Mass, in thanksgiving for Your favors, in reparation for my offenses, and in humble supplication for my temporal and eternal welfare, for the conversion of sinners, and for the relief of the poor souls in purgatory.

I wish to gain all the indulgences attached to the prayers I shall say and to the good works I shall perform this day.

Another Morning Offering

O JESUS, through the Immaculate Heart of Mary, I offer You my prayers, works, joys and sufferings of this day for all the intentions of Your Sacred Heart, in union with the Holy Sacrifice of the Mass throughout the world, in reparation for my sins, for the intentions of all our associates, and in particular for all the intentions of this month *(mention intention if known).*

Prayer for God's Protection and Christ's Presence

AS I arise today,
may the strength of God pilot me,
the power of God uphold me,
the wisdom of God guide me.
May the eye of God look before me,
the ear of God hear me,
the word of God speak for me.
May the hand of God protect me,
the way of God lie before me,
the shield of God defend me,
the host of God save me.
May Christ shield me today . . .
Christ with me, Christ before me,
Christ behind me,

Christ in me, Christ beneath me,
Christ above me,
Christ on my right, Christ on my left,
Christ when I lie down, Christ when I sit,
Christ when I stand,
Christ in the heart of everyone who thinks of me,
Christ in the mouth of everyone who speaks of me,
Christ in every eye that sees me,
Christ in every ear that hears me. (St. Patrick)

Midafternoon Prayer

O DIVINE Savior, I transport myself in spirit to Mount Calvary to ask pardon for my sins, for it was because of humankind's sins that You chose to offer Yourself in sacrifice. I thank You for Your extraordinary generosity and I am also grateful to You for making me a child of Mary, Your Mother.

Blessed Mother, take me under your protection. St. John, you took Mary under your care. Teach me true devotion to Mary, the Mother of God. May the Father, the Son, and the Holy Spirit be glorified in all places through the Immaculate Virgin Mary.

INVOCATIONS

May the Holy Trinity be blessed.

Christ conquers!
Christ reigns!
Christ commands!

O Heart of Jesus,
burning with love for us,
inflame our hearts with love for You.

O Heart of Jesus,
I place my trust in You.

O Heart of Jesus,
all for You.

Most Sacred Heart of Jesus,
have mercy on us.

Teach me to do Your will,
because You are my God. (Psalm 143:10)

Most Sacred Heart of Jesus,
have mercy on us.

O Lord,
increase our faith. (Luke 17:5)

Sweet Heart of Mary,
be my salvation.

Jesus, meek and humble of heart,
make my heart like unto Thine.

May the Most Blessed Sacrament be praised and adored forever.

Pray for us, O Holy Mother of God,
that we may be made worthy of the promises of Christ.

Father, into Your hands
I commend my spirit.

(Luke 23:46; see Psalm 31:6)

Merciful Lord Jesus,
grant them everlasting peace.

Queen conceived without original sin,
pray for us.

Holy Mother of God, Mary ever Virgin,
intercede for us.

Holy Mary,
pray for us.

My Jesus,
mercy.

EVENING PRAYERS

Prayer to the Blessed Trinity

I ADORE You, my God, and I thank You for having created me, for having made me a Christian and preserved me this day. I love You with all my heart and I am sorry for having sinned against You, because You are infinite Love and infinite Goodness. Protect me during my rest and may Your love be always with me. Amen.

Eternal Father, I offer You the Precious Blood of Jesus Christ in atonement for my sins and for all the intentions of our Holy Church.

Holy Spirit, Love of the Father and the Son, purify my heart and fill it with the fire of Your Love, so that I may be a chaste Temple of the Holy Trinity and be always pleasing to You in all things. Amen.

Plea for Divine Help

HEAR us, Lord, holy Father, almighty and eternal God; and graciously send Your holy angel from heaven to watch over, to cherish, to protect, to abide with, and to defend all who dwell in this house. Through Christ our Lord. Amen.

Prayer to Jesus

JESUS Christ, my God, I adore You and I thank You for the many favors You have bestowed on me this day. I offer You my sleep and all the moments of this night, and I pray You to preserve me from sin. Therefore, I place myself in Your most sacred Side, and under the mantle of our Blessed Lady, my Mother. May the holy angels assist me and keep me in peace, and may Your blessing be upon me.

Prayer for the Home

WE beseech You, O Lord, to visit this home, and to drive far from it all the snares of the enemy: let Your holy angels dwell therein so as to preserve us in peace; and let your blessing be always upon us. Through Christ our Lord. Amen.

Prayer to the Guardian Angel

ANGEL of God, my guardian dear, to whom His love entrusts me here, ever this night be at my side, to light and guard, to rule and guide. Amen.

Invocation to Jesus, Mary, and Joseph

JESUS, Mary, Joseph, I give You my heart and my soul. Jesus, Mary, Joseph, assist me in my last agony. Jesus, Mary, Joseph, may I sleep and rest in peace with You.

Our entire lives are lived in the loving embrace of Father, Son, and Holy Spirit.

PRAYERS FOR EVERY DAY OF THE WEEK

Sunday — The Most Holy Trinity

MOST blessed Trinity, Father, Son, and Holy Spirit, behold us kneeling in Your Divine presence. We humble ourselves deeply and beg of You the forgiveness of our sins.

We adore You, *almighty Father*, and with all our hearts we thank You for having given us Your Divine Son Jesus to be our Redeemer. He gave Himself to us in the Holy Eucharist even to the ends of the earth, and thus revealed to us the wondrous love of His heart in this mystery of faith and love.

We adore You, *Word of God*, dear Jesus our Redeemer, and with all our hearts we thank You for having taken human flesh upon Yourself and having become Priest and Victim for our redemption in the sacrifice of the Cross, a sacrifice that, through the great love of Your Sacred Heart, You renew upon our altars at every moment.

Give us the grace to honor Your Eucharistic Mystery with the devotion of Mary most holy and Your entire Church in heaven and on earth. We offer ourselves entirely to You. Accept it through Your infinite goodness and mercy; unite it to Your own and grant us Your blessing.

We adore You, *Divine Spirit,* and with all our hearts we thank You for having worked the unfathomable mystery of the Incarnation of the Word of God with such great love for us, a blessing that is being continually extended and increased in the Sacrament of the Eucharist. By this adorable mystery grant us and all poor sinners Your holy grace. Pour forth Your sacred gifts upon us and upon all redeemed souls.

Monday — The Holy Spirit

O HOLY Spirit, Divine Paraclete, Father of the poor, Consoler of the afflicted, and Sanctifier of souls, behold us prostrate in Your presence. We adore You with deepest submission and we repeat with the Seraphim who stand before Your throne: "Holy, holy, holy!"

You filled the soul of Mary with immense graces and inflamed the hearts of the Apostles with holy zeal; enkindle our hearts with Your love. You are a Divine Spirit; fortify us against evil spirits. You are a spiritual fire; set our hearts on fire with Your love. You are a supernatural light; enlighten us that we may understand eternal things. You appeared as a dove; grant us purity of life. You came as a wind full of sweetness; disperse the storms of passion that rise in us. You appeared as a tongue; teach us to sing Your praises without ceasing. You came forth in a cloud; cover us with the shade of Your protection.

O Bestower of heavenly gifts, vivify us by Your grace, sanctify us by Your love, and govern us by Your infinite mercy, so that we may never cease blessing, praising, and loving You now during our earthly lives and later in heaven for all eternity.

Tuesday — All Angels and Saints

HEAVENLY Father, in praising your Angels and Saints we praise Your glory, for by honoring them we honor You Who are their Creator. Their splendor shows us Your greatness, which surpasses that of all creation.

In Your loving Providence, You saw fit to send Your Angels to watch over us. Grant that we may always be under their protection and one day enjoy their company in heaven.

Heavenly Father, You are glorified in Your Saints, for their glory is the crowning of Your gifts. You provide an example for us by their lives on earth, You give us their friendship by our communion with them, You grant us strength and protection through their prayer for the Church, and You spur us on to victory over evil and the prize of eternal glory by this great company of witnesses. Grant that we who aspire to take part in their joy may be filled with the Spirit that blessed their lives, so that, after sharing their faith on earth, we may also experience their peace in heaven.

Help us to realize that there are Saints with whom we work day after day, with whom we live and take our leisure, with whom we come into contact every day. For whoever follows Your teachings faithfully and corresponds with Your grace is a living Saint. Help us to live in such a way as to attain this sanctity.

Wednesday — St. Joseph

HOLY Joseph, you were always most just; make us relish what is right. You sustained Jesus and Mary in time of trial; sustain us by your help. You provided for all the needs of Jesus and Mary; help the needy of the whole world. You rescued Jesus from

Herod when he sought to kill your child; save us from our many sins.

You were the foster father of Christ, the Priest-Victim; make priests faithful to their calling. You were the foster father of Christ, the Divine Physician; sustain the sick and obtain relief for them. You died the holiest of deaths in the arms of Jesus and Mary; intercede for the dying. You were the intrepid guardian of the Holy Family; protect all Christian families.

You cared for Jesus with true fatherly love; protect all children in the world. You were a dedicated and honest worker in your trade as a carpenter; teach us to labor for Jesus. You were the faithful and chaste spouse of the Blessed Virgin Mary; preserve in all hearts a love of fidelity and purity. You were a model single person and a model father later on; help all men to imitate your virtues.

Thursday — The Blessed Sacrament

LORD Jesus, at the Last Supper as You sat at table with Your Apostles, You offered Yourself to the Father as the spotless Lamb, the acceptable Gift that renders perfect praise to Him. You have given us the memorial of Your Passion to bring us its saving power until the end of time. In this great Sacrament You feed Your people and strengthen them in holiness, so that the human family may come to walk in the light of one faith, and in one communion of love. We are fed at Your table and grow into Your risen likeness.

Lord Jesus, You are the eternal and true Priest Who established this unending sacrifice. You offered Yourself as a Victim for our deliverance and You taught us to offer it throughout time in memory of You. As we eat Your Body that You gave for us, we grow in strength. As we drink Your Blood that You poured out for us, we are washed clean.

Lord Jesus, let the power of Your Eucharist pervade every aspect of our daily lives. Let Your consecration transform all our actions and all the events of each day into supernatural agents that form Your Mystical Body. Accept the bread of our efforts and the wine of our sufferings and sorrows. Transform all life that will spring up, grow, and flower this day and all death that will emerge to decrease and spoil. Grant that we may carry out the work You have given us to do and thus be united with You at every moment of our day.

Friday — The Holy Cross

LORD Jesus, from the height of Your throne of suffering You reveal the depth of Your love for us. Lifted up from the world on the Cross, You draw everyone to Yourself. The Cross is both the symbol and the act by which You raised up the world from all its sin and weakness. But You also ask for our cooperation.

Help us to die to self so that we may live for You and our fellow human beings. Set us free from the slavery of our passions, our prejudices, and our selfishness. Enable us to endure the pains and trials of this life and really help to change the world in our own small way.

Keep before our minds the conviction that in the Cross are salvation and life as well as defense against our enemies. Through the Cross heavenly grace is given us, our minds are strengthened, and we experience spiritual joy.

In the Cross is the height of virtue and the perfection of all sanctity. Let us take up our Cross, and follow You through earthly sorrow into eternal happiness in heaven.

Saturday — The Blessed Virgin Mary

O VIRGIN Mother of God, most august Mother of the Church, we commend the whole Church to you.

You bear the sweet name of "Help of Bishops"; keep the bishops in your care, and be at their side and at the side of the priests, religious, and laity who offer them help in sustaining the difficult work of the pastoral office.

From the Cross, the Divine Savior, your Son, gave you as a most loving Mother to the disciple whom He loved; remember the Christian people who commit themselves to you.

Be mindful of all your children; join to their prayers your special power and authority with God. Keep their faith whole and lasting, strengthen their hope, and enkindle their love.

Be mindful of those who find themselves in hardship, in need, in danger and especially those who are suffering persecution and are kept in chains because of their Christian faith. Ask for strength of soul for them, O Virgin Mother, and hasten the longed-for day of their liberation. Turn your eyes of mercy toward our separated brethren, and may it please you that one day we be joined together once again—you who gave birth to Christ, the Bridge and the Artisan of unity between God and human beings.

We commend the whole human race to your Immaculate Heart, O Virgin Mother of God. Lead it to acknowledge Jesus as the one true Savior. Drive far from it all the calamities provoked by sin. Bring it peace, which consists in truth, justice, liberty, and love.

By entrusting ourselves to Jesus in prayer we attain our true goal in life.

PRAYERS FOR EACH MONTH OF THE YEAR

January — The Most Holy Name of Jesus

MOST merciful Jesus, You began Your office of Savior by shedding Your Blood and assuming for us that Name which is above all names. I thank You for such early proofs of Your infinite love. I venerate Your sacred Name in union with the deep respect of the Angel who first announced it to the earth. I also unite my affections to the sentiments of tender devotion that Your adorable Name has in all ages enkindled in the hearts of Your servants.

Jesus, You said: "If You ask the Father anything in My Name, He will give it to you" (John 16:23). I earnestly ask the Father in Your Name for an increase of faith, hope, and love, and the grace to lead a good life and die a happy death.

Jesus, Your Name means "Savior." Be my Savior. Through Your adorable Name, which is the joy of heaven, the terror of hell, the consolation of the afflicted, and the solid ground of my unlimited confidence, grant me all the petitions I make in this prayer.

February — The Sacred Passion

DEAR Lord Jesus, by Your Passion and Resurrection You brought life to the world. But the glory of the Resurrection came only after the sufferings of the Passion.

You laid down Your life willingly and gave up everything for us. Your Body was broken and fastened to a Cross, Your clothing became the prize of soldiers, Your Blood ebbed slowly but surely away, and Your Mother was entrusted to the beloved disciple.

Stretched out on the Cross, deprived of all earthly possessions and human aid, racked with pain and burning with fever, You cried out to Your Father that the end had come. You had accomplished the work given You, and You committed into His hands, as a perfect gift, the little life that remained to You.

Lord, teach me to accept all afflictions after the example You have given. Let me place my death in Yours and my weakness in Your abandonment. Take hold of me with Your love—that same "foolish" love that knew no limits—and let me offer myself to the Father with You so that I may rise with You to eternal life.

March — St. Joseph

O GLORIOUS St. Joseph, you were chosen by God to be the foster father of Jesus, the most pure spouse of Mary ever Virgin, and the head of the holy family. You have been chosen by Christ's Vicar as the heavenly patron and protector of the Church founded by Christ. Therefore it is with great confidence that I implore your powerful assistance for the whole Church on earth. Protect in a special manner, with true fatherly love, the Pope and all bishops and priests in communion with the See of Peter. Be the protector of all who labor for souls amid the trials and tribulations of this life, and obtain that all the nations of the earth may docilely follow that Church out of which there is no salvation.

Dear St. Joseph, accept the offering of myself that I now make to you. I dedicate myself to your service, that you may ever be my father, my protector, and my guide in the way of salvation. Obtain for me great purity of heart and a fervent love for the interior life. May all my actions, after your example, be directed to the greater glory of God, in union with the Divine Heart of Jesus, the Immaculate Heart of Mary, and your own paternal heart. Finally, pray for me that I may share in the peace and joy of your holy death.

April — The Holy Eucharist

LORD Jesus, I believe that in the Holy Eucharist You give us the graces to enter into the mystery of Your redemptive sacrifice and to cooperate in the formation of the whole Christ. Grant me the grace of the spirit of sacrifice, a willingness to do whatever You ask of me, no matter what the cost.

With You I want to adore, love, and thank the heavenly Father from Whom comes every good gift. With You I beg the Supreme Judge to pardon my sins and those of Your people. With You I present my requests confidently because You have promised that the Father will give me whatever I ask in Your Name.

Jesus, help me to live the Mass, to bring its fruits into my everyday life. Give me the courage to be a Christ-bearer. Bearing You to my work and my leisure, I can make my daily tasks my Mass, and my whole life my thanksgiving. Help me to live out the Sacrifice of the Mass and carry You to the world.

May — The Blessed Virgin Mary

HOLIEST Virgin, with all my heart I venerate you above all the Angels and Saints in heaven as the daughter of the Eternal Father, and I consecrate to you my soul with all its powers.

Holiest Virgin, with all my heart I venerate you above all the Angels and Saints in heaven as the Mother of the only-begotten Son, and I consecrate to you my body with all its senses.

Holiest Virgin, with all my heart I venerate you above all the Angels and Saints in heaven as the beloved Spouse of the Holy Spirit, and I consecrate to you my heart with all its affections.

Holiest Virgin, intercede for me with the Holy Trinity that I may obtain the graces I need for my salvation. To you I entrust all my worries and miseries, my life and the end of my life, so that all my actions may be directed by the Divine Plan.

June — The Most Sacred Heart of Jesus

O LOVING Heart of our Lord Jesus Christ, You move hearts that are harder than rock, You melt spirits that are colder than ice, and You reach souls that are more impenetrable than diamonds. Touch my heart with Your Sacred Wounds and permeate my soul with Your Precious Blood, so that wherever I turn I will see only my Divine Crucified Lord, and everything I see will appear colored with Your Blood.

Lord Jesus, let my heart never rest until it finds You, Who are its Center, its Love, and its Happiness. By the Wound in Your Heart, pardon the sins that I have committed whether out of malice or out of evil desires. Place my weak heart in Your own Divine Heart, continually under Your protection and guidance, so that I may persevere in doing good and in fleeing evil until my last breath.

Heart of Jesus, save me.
Heart of my Creator, perfect me.
Heart of my Savior, deliver me.
Heart of my Judge, forgive me.
Heart of my Father, govern me.
Heart of my Spouse, love me.
Heart of my Master, teach me.
Heart of my King, crown me.
Heart of my Benefactor, enrich me.
Heart of my Pastor, defend me.
Heart of my Friend, embrace me.
Heart of my Infant Jesus, draw me.

Heart of Jesus dying on the Cross, pray for me.

Heart of Jesus, I greet You in all Your states. Give Yourself to me.

(St. Margaret Mary Alacoque)

July — The Precious Blood

PRECIOUS Blood of Jesus, infinite price of our redemption and both the drink and the laver of our souls, You continually plead the cause of all people before the throne of infinite mercy. From the depths of my heart I adore You. Jesus, insofar as I am able I want to make reparation for the insults and outrages that You receive from human beings, especially from those who blaspheme You.

Who would not venerate this Blood of infinite value! Who does not feel inflamed with love for Jesus Who shed it! What would have become of me had I not been redeemed by this Divine Blood! Who has drained It all from the veins of my Savior? Surely this was the work of love!

O infinite love, which has given us this saving balm! O balm beyond all price, welling up from the fountain of infinite love! Grant that every heart and every tongue may render You praise and thanks now and forever!

August — The Immaculate Heart of Mary

MARY, Mother of God, your heart is a shrine of holiness in which the demon of sin has never entered. After the Heart of Jesus, never was there a heart more pure and more holy. Your heart is a counterpart of the Heart of Jesus. His Heart is a loving Heart. Your heart is also the most affectionate of hearts after that of Jesus. You love as a mother loves her children. Your eyes ever watch over us; your ears constantly listen to our cries; your hands are always extended over us to help us and impart heavenly gifts; above all, your heart is full of tenderest care for us.

The heart of Jesus was a suffering Heart. Your heart was also a suffering heart. Its martyrdom began with Simeon's prophecy in the Temple and was completed on Calvary. When the hands and feet of Jesus were pierced with nails the sound of each blow of the hammer inflicted a wound in your heart. When His side was opened with a lance, a sword of sorrow also pierced your heart.

The Heart of Jesus was a pure Heart. Your heart was also a pure heart, free from the stain of original sin, and from the least stain of actual sin. Your heart is pure and spotless because it was sanctified beyond all other hearts by the indwelling of the Holy Spirit, making it worthy to be the dwelling place of the Sacred Heart of Jesus.

The Heart of Jesus was a generous Heart. Your heart is also a generous heart, full of love, abounding in mercy. All people may find a place there as your children if only they choose to heed your loving appeal. Your heart is a refuge for sinners, for you are the Mother of Mercy, who have never been known to turn away anyone who came to seek your aid.

I consecrate myself entirely to your Immaculate Heart. I give you my very being and my whole life: all that I have, all that I love, all that I am. I desire that all that is in me and around me may belong to you and may share in the benefits of your motherly blessing.

September — Our Lady, Queen of Martyrs

MARY, most holy Virgin, and Queen of Martyrs, accept the sincere homage of my childlike love. Welcome my poor soul into your heart pierced by so many sorrows. Receive it as the companion of your sorrows at the foot of the Cross, on which Jesus died for the redemption of the world. Sorrowful Virgin, in union with you I will gladly suffer all the trials, misunderstandings, and pains that our Lord lets me endure. I offer them all to you in memory of your sorrows, so that every thought of my mind and every beat of my heart may be an act of compassion and love for you.

Loving Mother, have pity on me and reconcile me to your Divine Son. Keep me in His grace and assist me in my last agony, so that I may be able to meet you in heaven and sing your glories.

Mary most sorrowful, Mother of Christians, pray for us. Mother of love, of sorrow, and of mercy, pray for us.

October — The Most Holy Rosary

MOST holy Virgin, you have revealed the treasures of graces hidden in the recitation of the Rosary. Inspire my heart with a sincere love for this devotion, so that by meditating on the mysteries of our redemption that are recalled in it, I may gather the fruits and obtain the special graces I ask of you, for the greater glory of God, for your honor, and for the good of my soul.

O Virgin Mary, grant that the recitation of the Rosary may be for me each day, amid my manifold duties, a bond of unity in my actions, a tribute of filial piety, a delightful refreshment, and an encouragement to walk joyfully along the path of my state in life. Let the mysteries of your Rosary form in me little by little a luminous atmosphere, pure, strengthening, and fragrant, which may penetrate my understanding and will, my heart and memory, my imagination and my whole being, so that I shall acquire the habit of praying while I work.

Most holy Virgin, obtain for me the grace of imitating the purity of your Annunciation, the charity of your Visitation, the tenderness of your love for Jesus born in a stable, the humility and obedience of your Presentation, so that we may merit also to find Jesus in the temple of glory after having sought Him eagerly on earth.

Blessed Virgin Mother, as I meditate upon the Luminous Mysteries, important events in the Public Ministry of your Son, help me to better understand my role in the Kingdom of God and encourage me to participate more fully in the grace of salvation to which I am called.

Sorrowful Virgin, teach me the Divine patience that associated you with the Passion of Jesus and made you co-redemptrix of the human race. Let me learn from you the way of Calvary, Christian resignation, and love of the Cross of your Divine Son.

Glorious Virgin, obtain for me that by meditating on the mysteries of your glorious and triumphant life, I may merit to be in heaven one day, among the ranks of your blessed servants, to render to you joint and eternal homage of filial love.

November — The Faithful Departed

CHRIST Jesus, Lord of life and Redeemer of the world, grant eternal rest to all the faithful departed. Let my relatives and friends whom You have called from this life attain their eternal home. Reward our departed benefactors with eternal blessedness. Grant Your departed priests and religious the recompense for their work in Your vineyard.

O Lord, receive into Your peace the souls of our brothers and sisters who labored for peace and justice on earth. Accept the sacrifices of those who gave their lives out of love for You and their fellow human beings. Look with mercy on all who showed goodwill to others, and grant them the peace they deserve.

O Lord, through the bloody Sweat that You suffered in the Garden of Gethsemane; through the pains that You suffered while carrying Your Cross to Calvary; through the pains that You suffered in Your most painful Crowning with Thorns; through the pains that You suffered during Your most cruel Crucifixion; through the pains that You suffered in Your most bitter agony on the Cross; through the immense pain that You suffered in breathing forth Your blessed soul; grant eternal rest to all the faithful departed.

December — The Holy Infancy

ADORABLE Child Jesus, in You wisdom resides, Divinity dwells, and all eternal riches are found. You are the beauty of heaven, the delight of the Angels, and the salvation of humankind. Here I am prostrated at Your feet, O Source of innocence, purity, and holiness. Although I am a slave of sin, I belong to You by the undeniable right of Your sovereignty.

I hereby render to You as my Lord—my King and my dignified and most adorable

Savior—my faith and my homage with the shepherds, and my act of adoration with the Magi. I give myself entirely and without restriction into Your powerful hands, which drew all the universe from nothingness and preserved it in the admirable order that we see.

O lovable Child, grant that as a result of my total devotion to honoring the mystery of Your Divine Childhood, I may have the happiness—through the mediation of Your holy Mother and St. Joseph, Your foster father—to live all the rest of my life in the same manner as You. May I live in You, for You, and under the direction of Your Divine Spirit, so that not one moment of my life deviates from Your Will, or forestalls it in any respect, but listens to it and faithfully follows it in every way.

PRAYERS FOR LITURGICAL TIMES

ADVENT

Prayer for Christ's Triple Coming

LAMB of God, You once came to rid the world of sin; cleanse me now of every stain of sin. Lord, You came to save what was lost; come once again with Your salvific power so that those You redeemed will not be punished. I have come to know You in faith; may I have unending joy when You come again in glory. Amen.

Prayer to Help Others Find Christ

O LORD Jesus, I thank You for the gift of faith and for the continual grace You give me to nourish and strengthen it. Enable me to cultivate the genuine desire for You that lies beneath the zealous search for justice, truth, love, and peace found in our contemporaries. Encourage these searchings, O Lord, and grant that all true seekers may look beyond the present moment and catch sight of Your countenance in the world. Amen.

CHRISTMAS TIME

Prayer to Jesus, God's Greatest Gift

O JESUS, I believe that the greatest proof of God's love is His gift to us of You, His only Son. All love tends to become like that which it loves. You love human beings; therefore You became Man. Infinite love and mercy caused You, the Second Person of the Blessed Trinity, to leave the Kingdom of eternal bliss, to descend from the throne of Your majesty, and to become a helpless babe. Eventually You even suffered and died and rose that we might live.

You wished to enter the world as a Child in order to show that You were true Man. But You became Man also that we may become like God. In exchange for the humanity that You take from us You wish to make us share in Your Divinity by sanctifying grace, so that You may take sole possession of us. Grant me the grace to love You in return with a deep, personal, and productive love. Amen.

Prayer for Christ's Rebirth in the Church

O LORD Jesus Christ, we ask You to incarnate in us Your invisible Divinity. What You accomplished corporally in Mary accomplish now spiritually in Your Church. May the Church's sure faith conceive You, its unstained intelligence give birth to You, and its soul united with the power of the Most High preserve You forever. Amen.

Prayer of Joy at the Birth of Jesus

LET the just rejoice, for their Justifier is born. Let the sick and infirm rejoice, for their Savior is born. Let captives rejoice, for their Redeemer is born. Let slaves rejoice, for their Master is born. Let free people rejoice, for their Liberator is born. Let all Christians rejoice, for Jesus Christ is born. Amen.

(St. Augustine of Hippo)

Prayer to Know and Love Jesus

MY LORD Jesus, I want to love You but You cannot trust me. If You do not help me, I will never do any good. I do not know You; I look for You but I do not find You. Come to me, O Lord. If I knew You, I would also know myself. If I have never loved You before, I want to love You truly now. I want to do Your will alone; putting no trust in myself, I hope in You, O Lord. Amen. (St. Philip Neri)

Prayer That Christ May Be Known to All

O LORD, give us a new Epiphany when You will be manifested to the world: to those who do not know You, to those who deny You, and to all those who unconsciously long for You. Bring the day closer when all people will know and love You together with the Father and the Holy Spirit—and the Kingdom of God will have arrived. Amen.

LENT

Prayer to Be Freed of the Seven Deadly Sins

O MEEK Savior and Prince of Peace, implant in me the virtues of gentleness and patience. Let me curb the fury of anger and restrain all resentment and impatience so as to overcome evil with good, attain Your peace, and rejoice in Your love.

O Model of humility, divest me of all pride and arrogance. Let me acknowledge my weakness and sinfulness, so that I may bear mockery and contempt for Your sake and esteem myself as lowly in Your sight.

O Teacher of abstinence, help me to serve You rather than my appetites. Keep me from gluttony—the inordinate love of food and drink—and let me hunger and thirst for Your justice.

O Lover of purity, remove all lust from my heart, so that I may serve You with a pure mind and a chaste body.

O Father of the poor, help me to avoid all covetousness for earthly goods and give me a love for heavenly things. Inspire me to give to the needy, just as You gave Your life that I might inherit eternal treasures.

O Exemplar of love, keep me from all envy and ill-will. Let the grace of Your love dwell in me that I may rejoice in the happiness of others and bewail their adversities.

O zealous Lover of souls, keep me from all sloth of mind or body. Inspire me with zeal for Your glory, so that I may do all things for You and in You. Amen.

Prayer of Contrition

MERCIFUL Father, I am guilty of sin. I confess my sins before You and I am sorry for them. Your promises are just; therefore I trust that You will forgive me my sins and cleanse me from every stain of sin. Jesus Himself is the propitiation for my sins and those of the whole world. I put my hope in His atonement. May my sins be forgiven through His Name, and in His Blood may my soul be made clean. Amen.

Prayer to Know Jesus Christ

O LORD Jesus, like St. Paul, may I count everything as loss in comparison with the supreme advantage of knowing You. I want to know You and what Your Passion and Resurrection can do. I also want to share in Your sufferings in the hope that if I resemble

You in death I may somehow attain to the resurrection from the dead.

Give me grace to make every effort to supplement faith with moral courage, moral courage with knowledge, knowledge with self-control, self-control with patience, patience with piety, piety with affection, and affection with love for all my brothers and sisters in Christ. May these virtues keep me both active and fruitful and bring me to the deep knowledge of You, Lord Jesus Christ. Amen.

Prayer to Appreciate the Mass

O LORD Jesus, in order that the merits of Your sacrifice on the Cross might be applied to every soul of all time, You willed that it should be renewed upon the altar. At the Last Supper, You said: "Do this in remembrance of Me." By these words You gave Your Apostles and their successors the power to consecrate and the command to do what You Yourself did.

I believe that the Mass is both a sacrifice and a memorial—reenacting Your Passion, Death, and Resurrection. Help me to realize that the Mass is the greatest gift of God to us and our greatest gift to God. Amen.

EASTER TIME

Prayer in Praise of Christ's Humanity

O RISEN Lord, Your Body was part of Your power, rather than You a part in Its weakness. For this reason You could not but rise again, if You were to die—because Your Body, once taken by You, never was or could be separated from You even in the grave.

I keep Your most holy Body before me as the pledge of my own resurrection. Though I die, it only means I shall rise again.

Teach me to live as one who believes in the great dignity and sanctity of the material frame that You have given to me. Amen.

Prayer for the Fruits of Christ's Resurrection

GOD, the Father of lights, You have glorified the world by the light of the risen Christ. Brighten my heart today with the light of Your faith. Through Your risen Son You opened the gate of eternal life for all human beings. Grant to me as I work out my salvation daily the hope of eternal life.

You accepted the sacrifice of Your Son and raised Him from the dead. Accept the offering of my work, which I perform for Your glory and the salvation of all people. Open my mind and heart to my brothers and sisters. Help us to love and serve one another.

Your Son rose to lift up the downtrodden, comfort the sorrowful, cure the sick, and bring joy to the world. Help all people to cast off sin and ignorance and enjoy Your Son's Paschal Victory. Amen.

Prayer to Christ Ascended into Heaven

O LORD Jesus, I adore You, Son of Mary, my Savior and my Brother, for You are God. I follow You in my thoughts, O first-fruits of our race, as I hope one day to follow You in my person into heavenly glory.

In the meantime, do not let me neglect the earthly task that You have given me. Let me labor diligently all my life with a greater appreciation for the present. Let me realize that only by accomplishing true human fulfillment can I attain Divine fulfillment and ascend to You at the completion of my work. Amen.

Prayer to Live a Full Life

O LORD, Your Ascension into heaven marks the culmination of the Paschal Mystery, and it contains an important teaching for us. We may live life as an earthly reality and develop our human potential to its fullest. We may make use of the results of science to achieve a better life on this planet. But in our best moments we know that there must be more than all of this, a transcending Reality.

As Christians, we know that this Reality is Your loving Father Who awaits us with You and the Holy Spirit. Where You have gone, we ultimately will come—if we are faithful. Amen.

Prayer to the Holy Spirit

HOLY Spirit of light and love, You are the substantial Love of the Father and the Son; hear my prayer.

Bounteous Bestower of most precious gifts, grant me a strong and living faith, which makes me accept all revealed truths and shape my conduct in accord with them. Give me a most confident hope in all Divine promises, which prompts me to abandon myself unreservedly to You and Your guidance.

Infuse into me a love of perfect goodwill, which makes me accomplish God's will in all things and act according to God's least desires. Make me love not only my friends but my enemies as well in imitation of Jesus Christ Who through You offered Himself on the Cross for all people. Holy Spirit, animate, inspire, and guide me, and help me to be always a true follower of Jesus. Amen.

ORDINARY TIME

Prayer for a Productive Faith

O LORD, increase my faith and let it bear fruit in my life. Let it bind me fast to other Christians in the common certitude that our Master is the God-Man Who gave His life for all. Let me listen in faith to the Divine word that challenges me.

Help me to strive wholeheartedly under the promptings of my faith in the building of a world ruled by love. Enable me to walk in faith toward the indescribable future that You have promised to all who possess a productive faith in You. Amen.

Prayer to Christ in the World

LORD Jesus, let us realize that every action of ours no matter how small or how secular enables us to be in touch with You. Let our interest lie in created things—but only in absolute dependence upon Your presence in them. Let us pursue You and You alone through the reality of created things. Let this be our prayer—to become closer to You by becoming more human.

Let us become a true branch on the vine that is You, a branch that bears much fruit. Let us accept You in our lives in the way it pleases

You to come into them: as Truth, to be spoken; as Life, to be lived; as Light, to be shared; as Love, to be followed; as Joy, to be given; as Peace, to be spread about; as Sacrifice, to be offered among our relatives and friends, among our neighbors and all people. Amen.

Prayer to Grow with the Church

O LORD Jesus, I know that all human relations take time if they are to grow and deepen. This is also true of my relations with You, the Father, and the Holy Spirit, which must grow over the course of my life.

But this growth is not automatic. Time means nothing unless I add my earnest efforts to it.

You have inspired Your Church to set aside special times when this growth can develop more intensely—the special Seasons of the Church Year. If I fail to move toward You during these times, I waste precious opportunities and endanger my spiritual life.

Help me to take them seriously and make a real attempt to use them well, so that I may grow into the person You want me to be. Amen.

Prayer to Encounter God Frequently in Prayer

HEAVENLY Father, let me realize that, like all prayer, prayer of petition is primarily a means of encountering You and being sustained by You. You know what we need because You are a loving Father Who watches over us. Yet You respect our freedom and wait for us to express our needs to You.

Let me have frequent recourse to You in prayer so that I will purify my intentions and bring my wishes into conformity with Your own. Let me pray with fixed formulas as well as in my own words—whether they be long or short.

Above all, let me come before You with a heart moved by Your Spirit and a will ready to conform to Your holy Will. Amen.

HOLY MASS—THE CHURCH'S GREATEST PRAYER

"AT the Last Supper, on the night when He was betrayed, our Savior instituted the Eucharistic sacrifice of His Body and Blood. He did this in order to perpetuate the sacrifice of the Cross throughout the centuries until He should come again, and so to entrust to His beloved Spouse, the Church, a memorial of His Death and Resurrection: a sacrament of love, a sign of unity, a bond of charity, a Paschal banquet in which Christ is eaten, the mind is filled with grace, and a pledge of future glory is given to us" (Vatican II: *Sacred Liturgy*, no. 47).

Thus the Mass is:

1) the *true sacrifice* of the New Covenant, in which a holy and living Victim is offered, Jesus Christ, and we in union with Him, as a gift of love and obedience to the Father;

2) a *sacred meal* and *spiritual banquet* of the children of God;

3) a *Paschal meal*, which evokes the passage (passover) of Jesus from this world to the Father; it renders Him present and makes Him live again in souls, and it anticipates our definitive passage to the Kingdom of God;

4) a *communitarian meal*, that is, a gathering together of the Head and His members, of Jesus and His Church, His Mystical Body, in order to carry out a perfect Divine worship.

Thus, the Mass is the greatest prayer we have. Through it we give thanks and praise to the Father for the wonderful future He has given us in His Son. We also ask forgiveness for our sins and beg the Father's blessing upon ourselves and our fellow human beings.

THE ORDER OF MASS

THE INTRODUCTORY RITES

Acts of prayer and penitence prepare us to meet Christ as he comes in word and sacrament. We gather as a worshiping community to celebrate our unity with him and with one another in faith.

STAND

Mass begins with an entrance procession of the ministers to the sanctuary, during which a chant is sung or the Entrance Antiphon of the day is recited.

GREETING (3 forms)

Priest: In the name of the Father, and of the Son, and of the Holy Spirit.

PEOPLE: **Amen.**

A ———

Priest: The grace of our Lord Jesus Christ,
and the love of God,
and the communion of the Holy Spirit
be with you all.

PEOPLE: **And with your spirit.**

B ——— OR ———

Priest: Grace to you and peace from God our Father
and the Lord Jesus Christ.

PEOPLE: **And with your spirit.**

C — OR —

Priest: The Lord be with you.

PEOPLE: And with your spirit.

PENITENTIAL ACT (3 forms)

Priest: Brethren (brothers and sisters), let us acknowledge our sins,
and so prepare ourselves to celebrate the sacred mysteries.

A —

Priest and **PEOPLE:**

I confess to almighty God
and to you, my brothers and sisters,
that I have greatly sinned,
in my thoughts and in my words,
in what I have done and in what I have failed to do,

And, striking their breast, they say:

through my fault, through my fault,
through my most grievous fault;

Then they continue:

therefore I ask blessed Mary ever-Virgin,
all the Angels and Saints,
and you, my brothers and sisters,
to pray for me to the Lord our God.

B — OR —

Priest: Have mercy on us, O Lord.

PEOPLE: For we have sinned against you.

Priest: Show us, O Lord, your mercy.

PEOPLE: **And grant us your salvation.**

C — OR —

Priest or other minister:

You were sent to heal the contrite of heart:
Lord, have mercy.

PEOPLE: **Lord, have mercy.**

Priest or other minister:

You came to call sinners:
Christ, have mercy.

PEOPLE: **Christ, have mercy.**

Priest or other minister:

You are seated at the right hand of the Father
to intercede for us:
Lord, have mercy.

PEOPLE: **Lord, have mercy.**

(Other invocations may be used.)

Absolution

At the end of any of the forms of the Penitential Act:

Priest: May almighty God have mercy on us,
forgive us our sins,
and bring us to everlasting life.

PEOPLE: **Amen.**

KYRIE

Unless included in the Penitential Act, the Kyrie is sung or said by all, with alternating parts for the choir or cantor and for the people.

℣. Lord, have mercy.

℟. **Lord, have mercy.**

℣. Christ, have mercy.

℟. **Christ, have mercy.**

℣. Lord, have mercy.

℟. **Lord, have mercy.**

GLORIA

As the Church assembled in the Spirit, we praise and pray to the Father and the Lamb.

GLORY to God in the highest,
and on earth peace to people of good will.

We praise you,
we bless you,
we adore you,
we glorify you,
we give you thanks for your great glory,
Lord God, heavenly King,
O God, almighty Father.

Lord Jesus Christ, Only Begotten Son,
Lord God, Lamb of God, Son of the Father,
you take away the sins of the world,
have mercy on us;

you take away the sins of the world,
receive our prayer;
you are seated at the right hand of the Father,
have mercy on us.

For you alone are the Holy One,
you alone are the Lord,
you alone are the Most High,
Jesus Christ,
with the Holy Spirit,
in the glory of God the Father.
Amen.

COLLECT

Priest: Let us pray.

The Priest and people pray silently for a while. Then the Priest says the Collect, which gives the theme of the particular celebration and asks God to help us. He concludes with the words:

. . . for ever and ever.

PEOPLE: **Amen.**

THE LITURGY OF THE WORD

The proclamation of God's Word is always centered on Christ, present through his Word. Old Testament writings prepare for him; New Testament books speak of him directly. All of scripture calls us to believe once more and to follow. After the reading we reflect upon God's words and respond to them.

SIT

READINGS AND RESPONSORIAL PSALM

At the end of the First Reading:

Reader: The word of the Lord.

PEOPLE: **Thanks be to God.**

The people repeat the response sung by the cantor the first time and then after each verse.

At the end of the Second Reading:

Reader: The word of the Lord.

PEOPLE: **Thanks be to God.**

ALLELUIA (Gospel Acclamation)

STAND

The people repeat the Alleluia after the cantor's Alleluia and then after the verse.

During Lent one of the following invocations is used as a response instead of the Alleluia:

(1) **Glory and praise to you, Lord Jesus Christ!**

(2) **Glory to you, Lord Jesus Christ, Wisdom of God the Father!**

(3) **Glory to you, Word of God, Lord Jesus Christ!**

(4) **Glory to you, Lord Jesus Christ, Son of the Living God!**

(5) **Praise and honor to you, Lord Jesus Christ!**

(6) **Praise to you, Lord Jesus Christ, King of endless glory!**

(7) **Marvelous and great are your works, O Lord!**

(8) **Salvation, glory, and power to the Lord Jesus Christ!**

GOSPEL

Deacon (or Priest): The Lord be with you.

PEOPLE: **And with your spirit.**

Deacon (or Priest):

✠ A reading from the holy Gospel according to N.

PEOPLE: **Glory to you, O Lord.**

At the end:

Deacon (or Priest): The Gospel of the Lord.

PEOPLE: **Praise to you, Lord Jesus Christ.**

HOMILY

SIT

God's Word is spoken again in the Homily. The Holy Spirit speaking through the lips of the preacher explains and applies today's biblical readings to the needs of this particular congregation. He calls us to respond to Christ through the life we lead.

PROFESSION OF FAITH (CREED)

As a people we express our acceptance of God's message in the Scriptures and the Homily. We summarize our faith by proclaiming a creed handed down from the early Church.

All say the Profession of Faith on Sundays and Solemnities.

THE NICENE CREED

STAND

I believe in one God,
the Father almighty,
maker of heaven and earth,
of all things visible and invisible.

I believe in one Lord Jesus Christ,
the Only Begotten Son of God,
born of the Father before all ages.
God from God, Light from Light,
true God from true God,
begotten, not made, consubstantial with the Father;
through him all things were made.
For us men and for our salvation
he came down from heaven,

At the words that follow, up to and including **and became man***, all bow.*

and by the Holy Spirit was incarnate of the Virgin Mary,
and became man.

For our sake he was crucified under Pontius Pilate,
he suffered death and was buried,
and rose again on the third day
in accordance with the Scriptures.

He ascended into heaven
and is seated at the right hand of the Father.
He will come again in glory
to judge the living and the dead
and his kingdom will have no end.

I believe in the Holy Spirit, the Lord, the giver of life,
who proceeds from the Father and the Son,
who with the Father and the Son is adored and glorified,
who has spoken through the prophets.

I believe in one, holy, catholic and apostolic Church.
I confess one Baptism for the forgiveness of sins
and I look forward to the resurrection of the dead
and the life of the world to come. Amen.

OR:

THE APOSTLES' CREED

In celebration of Masses with children, the Apostles' Creed may be said after the Homily.

I BELIEVE in God,
the Father almighty,
Creator of heaven and earth,
and in Jesus Christ, his only Son, our Lord,

At the words that follow, up to and including the Virgin Mary*, all bow.*

who was conceived by the Holy Spirit,
born of the Virgin Mary,
suffered under Pontius Pilate,
was crucified, died and was buried;
he descended into hell;
on the third day he rose again from the dead;
he ascended into heaven,
and is seated at the right hand of God the Father almighty;
from there he will come to judge the living and the dead.

I believe in the Holy Spirit,
the holy catholic Church,
the communion of saints,
the forgiveness of sins,
the resurrection of the body,
and life everlasting. Amen.

THE UNIVERSAL PRAYER

(Prayer of the Faithful)

As a priestly people we unite with one another to pray for today's needs in the Church and the world.

After the Priest's introduction the Deacon or other minister sings or says the invocations.

PEOPLE: **Lord, hear our prayer.**

(or other response, according to local custom)
At the end the Priest says the concluding prayer:

PEOPLE: **Amen.**

THE LITURGY OF THE EUCHARIST

Made ready by reflection on God's Word, we enter now into the eucharistic sacrifice itself, the Supper of the Lord. We celebrate the memorial which the Lord instituted at his Last Supper. We are God's new people, the redeemed brothers and sisters of Christ, gathered by him around his table. We are here to bless God and to receive the gift of Jesus' Body and Blood so that our faith and life may be transformed.

PREPARATION OF THE GIFTS

SIT

The bread and wine for the Eucharist, with our gifts for the Church and the poor, are gathered and brought to the altar. We prepare our hearts by song or in silence as the Lord's table is being set.

PREPARATION OF THE BREAD

Blessed are you, Lord God of all creation,
for through your goodness we have received
the bread we offer you:
fruit of the earth and work of human hands,
it will become for us the bread of life.

If there is no singing, the Priest may say this prayer aloud, and the people may acclaim:

PEOPLE: **Blessed be God for ever.**

PREPARATION OF THE WINE

By the mystery of this water and wine
may we come to share in the divinity of Christ
who humbled himself to share in our humanity.

Blessed are you, Lord God of all creation,
for through your goodness we have received
the wine we offer you:
fruit of the vine and work of human hands,
it will become our spiritual drink.

If there is no singing, the Priest may say this prayer aloud, and the people may acclaim:

PEOPLE: **Blessed be God for ever.**

INVITATION TO PRAYER

Priest: Pray, brethren (brothers and sisters),
that my sacrifice and yours
may be acceptable to God,
the almighty Father.

STAND

PEOPLE: **May the Lord accept the sacrifice at your hands**
for the praise and glory of his name,
for our good
and the good of all his holy Church.

The Priest, speaking in our name, says the Prayer over the Offerings, asking the Father to bless and accept these offerings.

PEOPLE: **Amen.**

EUCHARISTIC PRAYER

Priest: The Lord be with you.

PEOPLE: **And with your spirit.**

Priest: Lift up your hearts.

PEOPLE: **We lift them up to the Lord.**

Priest: Let us give thanks to the Lord our God.

PEOPLE: **It is right and just.**

The Priest says the Preface here.

HOLY, HOLY, HOLY

Priest and PEOPLE:

Holy, Holy, Holy Lord God of hosts.
Heaven and earth are full of your glory.
Hosanna in the highest.
Blessed is he who comes in the name of the Lord.
Hosanna in the highest.

KNEEL

MEMORIAL ACCLAMATION

Priest: The mystery of faith.

PEOPLE:

A **We proclaim your Death, O Lord,**
and profess your Resurrection
until you come again.

B **When we eat this Bread and drink this Cup,**
we proclaim your Death, O Lord,
until you come again.

C **Save us, Savior of the world,**
for by your Cross and Resurrection
you have set us free.

GREAT AMEN

Priest: . . . for ever and ever.

PEOPLE: **Amen.**

THE COMMUNION RITE

To prepare for the paschal meal, to welcome the Lord, we pray for forgiveness and exchange a sign of peace. Before eating Christ's Body and drinking his Blood, we must be one with him.

STAND

THE LORD'S PRAYER

The Priest asks the people to join him in the prayer that Jesus taught us.

Priest and **PEOPLE:**

OUR Father, who art in heaven,
hallowed be thy name;
thy kingdom come,
thy will be done
on earth as it is in heaven.

Give us this day our daily bread,
and forgive us our trespasses,
as we forgive those who trespass against us;
and lead us not into temptation,
but deliver us from evil.

DOXOLOGICAL CONCLUSION AND ACCLAMATION

Priest: Deliver us, Lord, we pray, from every evil,
graciously grant peace in our days,
that, by the help of your mercy,
we may be always free from sin
and safe from all distress,
as we await the blessed hope
and the coming of our Savior, Jesus Christ.

PEOPLE: **For the kingdom,**
the power and the glory are yours
now and for ever.

SIGN OF PEACE

The Priest says the prayer for peace:

LORD Jesus Christ,
who said to your Apostles:
Peace I leave you, my peace I give you,
look not on our sins,
but on the faith of your Church,

and graciously grant her peace and unity
in accordance with your will.
Who live and reign for ever and ever.

PEOPLE: **Amen.**

Priest: The peace of the Lord be with you always.

PEOPLE: **And with your spirit.**

Deacon (or Priest):
Let us offer each other the sign of peace.

The people exchange a sign of peace and charity, according to local custom.

LAMB OF GOD

The Priest breaks the host over the paten and places a small piece in the chalice, saying quietly:

May this mingling of the Body and Blood
of our Lord Jesus Christ
bring eternal life to us who receive it.

Meanwhile the following is sung or said:

PEOPLE:

Lamb of God, you take away the sins of the world,
have mercy on us.
Lamb of God, you take away the sins of the world,
have mercy on us.

Lamb of God, you take away the sins of the world,
grant us peace.

***The invocation may be repeated until the breaking of the bread is finished, but the last phrase is always:* "Grant us peace."**

KNEEL

The Priest prays quietly before Communion.

INVITATION TO COMMUNION

The Priest genuflects. Holding the host elevated slightly over the paten, the Priest says:

Priest: Behold the Lamb of God,
behold him who takes away the sins of the world.
Blessed are those called to the supper of the Lamb.

Priest and **PEOPLE** *(once only):*
Lord, I am not worthy
that you should enter under my roof,
but only say the word
and my soul shall be healed.

Priest: The Body of Christ.

Communicant: **Amen.**

Priest: The Blood of Christ.

Communicant: **Amen.**

The Communion Chant or other appropriate song or hymn is sung while Communion is given to the faithful. If there is no singing, the Communion Antiphon is said.

STAND

PRAYER AFTER COMMUNION

Then, in the Prayer after Communion, the Priest prays in our name that we may live the life of faith since we have been strengthened by Christ himself. Our *Amen* makes his prayer our own.

Priest: Let us pray. . . .

PEOPLE: **Amen.**

THE CONCLUDING RITES

We have heard God's Word and eaten the Body of Christ. Now it is time for us to leave, to do good works, to praise and bless the Lord in our daily lives.

STAND

BLESSING AND DISMISSAL

Priest: The Lord be with you.

PEOPLE: **And with your spirit.**

Priest:

May almighty God bless you,
the Father, and the Son, ✠ and the Holy Spirit.

PEOPLE: **Amen.**

Deacon (or Priest):

A Go forth, the Mass is ended.

B God and announce the Gospel of the Lord.

C Go in peace, glorifying the Lord by your life.

D Go in peace.

PEOPLE: **Thanks be to God.**

COMMUNION PRAYERS

THE Eucharist is not only a Sacrifice but a spiritual banquet as well. Jesus renews His immolation in Holy Mass and gives us Himself as our spiritual nourishment (Jn 6:54-55).

Communion is the most perfect participation in the Eucharistic Sacrifice and its most logical conclusion.

The Divine effects that Communion produces in souls will be so much more complete and enduring the more fervently one prepares and offers thanksgiving for Communion.

Indeed, "union with Christ, to which the Sacrament itself is directed, is not to be limited to the duration of the celebration of the Eucharist; it is to be prolonged into the entire Christian life, in such a way that the Christian faithful, contemplating unceasingly the gift they have received, may make their life a continual thanksgiving under the guidance of the Holy Spirit and may produce fruits of greater charity" *(Instruction on the Eucharistic Mystery*, no. 38).

PRAYERS BEFORE HOLY COMMUNION

Act of Hope

GOOD Jesus, in You alone I place all my hope. You are my salvation and my strength, the Source of all good. Through Your mercy, through Your Passion and Death, I hope to obtain the pardon of my sins, the grace of final perseverance and a happy eternity.

Act of Love

JESUS, my God, I love You with my whole heart and above all things, because You are the one supreme Good and an infinitely perfect Being. You have given Your life for me, a poor sinner, and in Your mercy You have even offered Yourself as Food for my soul.

My God, I love You. Inflame my heart to love You more.

Act of Contrition

O MY Savior, I am truly sorry for having offended You because You are infinitely good and sin displeases You. I detest all the sins of my life and I desire to atone for them. Through the merits of Your Precious Blood, wash from my soul all stain of sin, so that, cleansed in body and soul, I may worthily approach the Most Holy Sacrament of the Altar.

Act of Desire

JESUS, my God and my all, my soul longs for You. My heart yearns to receive You in Holy Communion. Come, Bread of heaven and Food of angels, to nourish my soul and to rejoice my heart. Come, most lovable Friend of my soul, to inflame me with such love that I may never again be separated from You.

Prayer of St. Thomas Aquinas

ALMIGHTY and eternal God, I approach the Sacrament of Your only-begotten Son, our Lord Jesus Christ. As a sick man I approach the physician of life; as a man unclean, I come to the fountain of mercy; blind, to the light of eternal brightness; poor and needy, to the Lord of heaven and earth. I beseech You, therefore, in Your boundless mercy, to heal my sickness, to wash away my defilements, to enlighten my blindness, to enrich my poverty, and to clothe my nakedness.

Let me receive the Bread of angels, the King of kings, the Lord of lords, with such reverence and humility, such contrition and faith, such purpose and intention, as may help the salvation of my soul. Grant, I beseech You, that I may receive not only the Sacrament of the Body and Blood of our Lord, but also the whole grace and virtue of the Sacrament.

O most indulgent God, grant me so to receive the Body of Your only-begotten Son, our Lord Jesus Christ, which He took of the Virgin Mary, that I may be found worthy to be incorporated with His Mystical Body and numbered among His members.

O most loving Father, grant that I may one day forever contemplate Him unveiled and face to face, Whom, on my pilgrimage, I receive under a veil, Your beloved Son, Who lives and reigns with You and the Holy Spirit, one God, forever and ever.

PRAYERS AFTER HOLY COMMUNION

Act of Faith

JESUS, I firmly believe that You are present within me as God and Man, to enrich my soul with graces and to fill my heart with the happiness of the blessed. I believe that You are Christ, the Son of the living God!

Act of Adoration

WITH deepest humility, I adore You, my Lord and God; You have made my soul Your dwelling place. I adore You as my Creator from Whose hands I came and with Whom I long to be happy forever.

Act of Love

DEAR Jesus, I love You with my whole heart, my whole soul, and with all my strength. May the love of Your own Sacred Heart fill my soul and purify it so that I may die to the world for love of You, as You died on the Cross for love of me. My God, You are all mine; grant that I may be all Yours in time and in eternity.

Act of Thanksgiving

FROM the depths of my heart I thank You, dear Lord, for Your infinite kindness in coming to me. How good You are to me! With Your most holy Mother and all the angels, I praise Your mercy and generosity toward me, a poor sinner. I thank You for nourishing my soul with Your Sacred Body and Precious Blood. I will try to show my gratitude to You in the Sacrament of Your love, by obedience to Your holy Commandments, by fidelity to my duties, by kindness to my neighbor and by an earnest endeavor to become like You in my daily conduct.

Prayer to Christ the King

O CHRIST Jesus, I acknowledge You as King of the universe. All that has been created has been made for You. Exercise upon me all Your rights. I renew my baptismal promises, renouncing Satan and all his works and pomps. I promise to live a good Christian life and to be diligent in furthering the interests and teachings of Almighty God and Your Church.

Prayer of St. Thomas Aquinas

I THANK You, O holy Lord, almighty Father, eternal God, Who have deigned, not through any merit of mine, but out of the condescension of Your goodness, to nourish me, a sinner, Your unworthy servant, with the Precious Body and Blood of Your Son, our Lord Jesus Christ.

I pray that this Holy Communion be not a condemnation to punishment for me, but a saving plea unto forgiveness.

May it be unto me the armor of faith and the shield of a good will. May it be the emptying out of my vices and the extinction of all lustful desires; an increase of charity and patience, of humility and obedience, and of all virtues; a strong defense against the snares of all my enemies, visible and invisible; the perfect quieting of all my evil impulses of flesh and spirit, binding me firmly to You, the one true God; and a happy ending of my life.

I pray too that You will deign to bring me, a sinner, to that ineffable banquet, where You, with Your Son and the Holy Spirit, are to Your Saints true light, fulfillment of desires, eternal joy, gladness without end, and perfect bliss. Through Christ our Lord.

Prayer to Our Redeemer

SOUL of Christ, sanctify me.
Body of Christ, save me.
Water from the side of Christ, wash me.
Blood of Christ, motivate me.
Passion of Christ, strengthen me.
O good Jesus, hear me.
Within Your wounds, hide me.
Suffer me not to be separated from You.
From the malignant enemy, defend me.
At the hour of death, call me,
And bid me come to You,
That with Your Saints I may praise You
Forever and ever.

Prayer to Jesus Christ Crucified

BEHOLD, O kind and most sweet Jesus, I cast myself upon my knees in Your sight, and with the most fervent desire of my soul I pray and beseech You that You would impress upon my heart lively sentiments of Faith, Hope, and Charity, with true repentance for my sins, and a firm desire of amendment, while with deep affection and grief of soul I ponder within myself and mentally contemplate Your five most precious wounds, having before my eyes that which David spoke in prophecy of You, O good Jesus: They have pierced my hands and feet; they have numbered all my bones.

A *plenary indulgence* is granted on each Friday of Lent and Passiontide to the faithful, who after Communion piously recite the above prayer before an image of Christ crucified; on other days of the year the indulgence is *partial.*

Prayer to Jesus and Mary

O JESUS, living in Mary, come and live in Your servants, in the spirit of Your holiness, in the fullness of Your power, in the perfection of Your ways, and in the truth of Your mysteries. Reign in us over all adverse power through Your Holy Spirit, and for the glory of the Father. Amen.

Mary, I come to you with childlike confidence and earnestly beg you to take me under your powerful protection. Grant me a place in your loving motherly heart. I place my immortal soul into your hands and give you my own poor heart.

Prayer to St. Joseph

GUARDIAN of virgins, and holy father Joseph, to whose faithful custody Christ Jesus, Innocence itself, and Mary, Virgin of virgins, were committed: I beg you, by these dear pledges, Jesus and Mary, that, being preserved from all uncleanness, I may with spotless mind, pure heart and chaste body ever serve Jesus and Mary most chastely all the days of my life. Amen.

VISITS TO THE BLESSED SACRAMENT

THROUGHOUT the course of the day we should strive to spend a few moments before Jesus in the Blessed Sacrament of the Altar. We should adore and thank Him for all the gifts that He has given us and for the gift of His Real Presence, then tell Him our needs and everything that is in our heart, so that we may receive comfort and strength.

The tabernacle is the Font of grace and mercy from which Jesus dispenses the benefit of His superabundant life and continually repeats to all: "Come to Me, all you who are weary and overburdened, and I will give you rest" (Mt 11:28).

The Eucharist is the sign of God's great love for us and fills us with happiness and gratitude. At the same time, it fills us with sorrow and pain because God's love is not returned by His people. The Heart that has so loved human beings remains neglected and even offended by them.

Conscious of this sad situation, we should make reparation for ourselves and for others. To make reparation signifies being united to Christ, taking up our cross and carrying it out of love for Him in atonement. Then our human love will dimly resemble Divine love, becoming an eternal, universal, and saving love.

Act of Adoration

WE adore You, Most Holy Lord, Jesus Christ, here and in all the churches of the whole world, and we bless You because by Your holy Cross You have redeemed the world. Have mercy on us.

(St. Francis of Assisi)

Prayer of Adoration and Petition

I ADORE You, O Jesus, true God and true Man, here present in the Holy Eucharist, as I humbly kneel before You and unite myself in spirit with all the faithful on earth and all the Saints in heaven.

In heartfelt gratitude for so great a blessing, I love You, my Jesus, with my whole soul, for You are infinitely perfect and all worthy of my love. Give me the grace never more in any way to offend You. Grant that I may be renewed by Your Eucharistic presence here on earth and be found worthy to arrive with Mary at the enjoyment of Your eternal and blessed presence in heaven.

Prayer of Reparation

WITH that deep and humble feeling which the Faith inspires in me, O my God and Savior, Jesus Christ, true God and true Man, I love You with all my heart, and I adore You Who are hidden here. I do so in reparation for all the irreverences, profanations, and sacrileges that You receive in the most august Sacrament of the Altar.

I adore You, O my God, but not so much as You are worthy to be adored. Please accept my goodwill and help me in my weakness. Would that I could adore You with that perfect worship which the angels in heaven are able to offer You. O Jesus, may You be adored, loved, and thanked by all people at every moment in this most holy Sacrament.

Prayer for Today's Needs

LORD, for tomorrow and its needs I do not pray;
keep me, my God, from stain of sin, just for today.
Let me both diligently work and duly pray;
let me be kind in word and deed, just for today.
Let me be slow to do my will, prompt to obey;

help me to mortify my flesh, just for today.
Let me no wrong or idle word unthinking say;
set a seal upon my lips, just for today.
Let me in season, Lord, be grave, in season gay;
let me be faithful to Your grace, just for today.
And if today my tide of life should ebb away,
give me Your Sacraments divine, sweet Lord, today.
So for tomorrow and its needs, I do not pray;
but keep me, guide me, love me, Lord, just for today.

(Sister M. Xavier, S.N.D.)

Prayer to Bring Christ into Our Day

LORD Jesus, present before me in the Sacrament of the Altar, help me to cast out from my mind all thoughts of which You do not approve and from my heart all emotions that You do not encourage. Enable me to spend my entire day as a co-worker with You, carrying out the tasks that You have entrusted to me.

Be with me at every moment of this day: during the long hours of work, that I may never tire or slacken from Your service; during my conversations, that they may not become for me occasions for meanness toward others; during the moments of worry and stress, that I may remain patient and spiritually calm; during periods of fatigue and illness, that I may avoid self-pity and think of others; during times of temptation, that I may take refuge in Your grace.

Help me to remain generous and loyal to You this day and so be able to offer it all up to You with its successes, which I have achieved by Your help and its failures, which have occurred through my own fault. Let me come to the wonderful realization that life is most real when it is lived with You as the Guest of my soul.

Invocations

PRAISE and adoration ever more be given to the most Holy Sacrament.

O SACRAMENT most holy, O Sacrament Divine! All praise and all thanksgiving be every moment Thine!

We behold Christ crucified, He Who died for our sins.

THE STATIONS OF THE CROSS

THE Stations of the Cross is a devotion to the Sacred Passion, in which we accompany, in spirit, our Blessed Lord in His sorrowful journey from the house of Pilate to Calvary, and meditate on His sufferings and death.

Before each Station genuflect and say: "We adore You, O Christ, and we bless You; because by Your holy Cross, You have redeemed the world." Then meditate upon the scene before you for a few moments. The short prayers for each Station may be helpful.

1. Jesus Is Condemned to Death

O Jesus, You desired to die for me that I may receive supernatural life, sanctifying grace, and become a child of God. How precious must be that life. Teach me to appreciate it more and help me never to lose it by sin.

2. Jesus Bears His Cross

O Jesus, You have chosen to die the disgraceful death on the Cross. You have paid a high price for my redemption and the life of grace that was bestowed upon me. May I love You always and bear my crosses for Your sake.

3. Jesus Falls the First Time

O Jesus, Your painful fall under the Cross and Your quick rise teach me to repent and rise instantly should I ever be forgetful of Your love and commit a mortal sin. Make me strong enough to conquer my wicked passions.

4. Jesus Meets His Mother

O Jesus, Your afflicted Mother was resigned to Your Passion because she is my Mother also, and wants to see me live and die as a child of God. Grant me a tender love for You and Your holy Mother.

5. Jesus Is Helped by Simon

O Jesus, Simon first reluctantly helped You to carry the Cross. Make me better understand the value of my sufferings which should lead me closer to You, as Simon was united with You through the Cross.

6. Jesus and Veronica

O Jesus, how graciously did You reward that courageous woman. When I side with You against sin and temptation, You surely will increase the beauty of my soul and fill me with joy and peace. Jesus, give me courage.

7. Jesus Falls a Second Time

O Jesus, despite my good resolutions I have sinned repeatedly. But Your sufferings assure me of forgiveness if only I return to You with a contrite heart. I repent for having offended You. Help me to avoid sin in the future.

8. Jesus Speaks to the Women

O Jesus, You told the women of Jerusalem to weep for their sins rather than for You. Make me weep for my sins which caused Your terrible sufferings and the loss of my friendship with You.

9. Jesus Falls a Third Time

O Jesus, I see You bowed to the earth, enduring the pains of extreme exhaustion. Grant that I may never yield to despair in time of hardship and spiritual distress. Let me come to You for help and comfort.

10. Jesus Is Stripped of His Garments

O Jesus, You permitted Yourself to be stripped of Your garments. Strip me of sin and clothe me with Your holiness. Grant that I may sacrifice all my unlawful attachments rather than imperil the divine life of my soul.

11. Jesus Is Nailed to the Cross

O Jesus, how could I complain if nailed to God's Commandments, which are given for my salvation, when I see You nailed to the Cross! Strengthen my faith and increase my love for You. Help me keep the Commandments.

12. Jesus Dies on the Cross

O Jesus, dying on the Cross, You preached love and forgiveness. May I be thankful that You have made me a child of God. Help me to forgive all who have injured me, so that I myself may obtain forgiveness.

13. Jesus Is Taken from the Cross

O Jesus, a sword of grief pierced Your Mother's heart when You were lying lifeless in her arms. Grant me through her intercession to lead the life of a loyal child of Mary, so that I may be received by her at my death.

14. Jesus Is Placed in the Sepulcher

O Jesus, Your enemies triumphed when they sealed Your tomb. But Your eternal triumph began on Easter morning. Strengthen my goodwill to live for You until the divine life of my soul will be manifested in heaven.

THE PSALMS: PRAYERBOOK OF THE HOLY SPIRIT

THE Psalms are the prayer of God's assembly, the public prayer par excellence of the People of God. No prayer of Israel is comparable to the Psalter because of its universal character. The idea of the unity of the Chosen People's prayer guided its elaboration as well as its adoption by the Church.

In giving us the Psalter, which sums up the major aspects of our relationship to our Creator and Redeemer, God puts into our mouths the words He wishes to hear, and indicates to us the dimensions of prayer.

"The Psalms recall to mind the truths revealed by God to the Chosen People, which were at one time frightening and at another filled with wonderful tenderness; they keep repeating and fostering the hope of the promised Redeemer, which in ancient times was kept alive with song, either around the hearth or in the stately temple; they show forth in splendid light the prophesied glory of Jesus Christ: first, His supreme and eternal power, then His lowly coming to this earthly exile, His kingly dignity and priestly power, and finally His beneficent labors, and the shedding of His Blood for our redemption.

"In a similar way they express the joy, the bitterness, the hope and fear of our hearts and our desire of loving God and hoping in Him alone, and our mystic ascent to divine tabernacles" (Pope Pius XII, *Mediator Dei*, no. 148).

In short, the Psalms constitute an inexhaustible treasury of prayers for every occasion and mood in a format that is true to the whole tradition of the History of Salvation.

Prayer for True Happiness

The way of the just

BLESSED is the man
who does not walk in the counsel of the wicked,
nor stand in the way of sinners,
nor sit in the company of scoffers.
Rather, his delight is in the law of the Lord,
and on that law he meditates day and night.

He is like a tree planted near streams of water,
which bears fruit in its season,
and whose leaves never wither.
In the same way,
everything he does will prosper.

The way of the sinner

This is not true of the wicked,
for they are like chaff that the wind blows away.
Therefore, the wicked will not stand firm at the judgment,
nor sinners in the assembly of the righteous.

For the Lord watches over the way of the righteous,
but the way of the wicked will perish.

(Psalm 1)

Prayer of Trust in God

A call for God's help

WHEN I call upon You, answer me, O God,
You Who uphold my rights.
When I was in distress, You set me free;
have pity on me and listen to my prayer.

Sinner, repent

How long will you people turn My glory into shame,
cherishing what is worthless and pursuing what is false?
Remember that the Lord wonderfully favors those who are faithful,
and the Lord listens when I call out to Him.

When you are angry, be careful not to sin;
reflect in silence
as you lie upon your beds.
Offer worthy sacrifices
and place your trust in the Lord.

Confidence in God

Many exclaim, "Who will show us better times!
Let the light of Your face shine on us, O Lord!"
You have granted my heart greater joy
than others experience when grain and wine abound.
In peace I lie down and sleep,
for only with Your help, O Lord,
can I rest secure.

(Psalm 4)

Prayer for Divine Assistance

A call for help

LISTEN to my words, O Lord;
pay heed to my sighs.
Hear my cry for help,
my King and my God;
for to You I pray.

O Lord, at daybreak You hear my voice;
at daybreak I bring my petition before You
and await Your reply.

Hatred of evil

For You are not a God Who delights in wickedness;
evil cannot remain in Your presence.
The arrogant shrink before Your gaze;
You hate all who do evil.
You destroy all who tell lies;
the Lord detests the violent and the deceitful.

Guidance

But I will enter Your house
because of Your great kindness,
and I will bow down in Your holy temple,
filled with awe of You.
Lead me in Your ways of righteousness, O Lord,

for I am surrounded by enemies;
make Your path straight before me.

Destruction of the wicked

For there is nothing trustworthy in their mouth;
their heart devises treacherous schemes.
Their throat is a wide open grave;
with their tongue they utter flattery.
Punish them, O God;
may their intrigues result in their downfall.
Cast them out because of their many transgressions,
for they have rebelled against You.

Protection of the just

But may all who take refuge in You rejoice;
may they shout for joy forever.
Grant them Your protection
so that those who love Your name may rejoice in You.
Truly, You bless the righteous, O Lord;
You surround them with Your goodwill as with a shield.

(Psalm 5)

Prayer of Repentance

Sorrow for sin

O LORD, do not rebuke me in Your anger
or punish me in Your wrath.
Have mercy on me, O Lord, for I am tottering;
help me, O Lord, for my body is in agony.
My soul is also filled with anguish.
But You, O Lord—how long?

The mercy of God

Turn, O Lord, and deliver my soul;
save me because of Your kindness.
For among the dead who remembers You?
In the netherworld who sings Your praises?

I am exhausted from my sighing;
every night I flood my bed with my tears,
and I soak my couch with my weeping.
My eyes grow dim because of my grief;
they are worn out because of all my foes.

Confidence in prayer

Depart from me, all you evildoers,
for the Lord has heard the sound of my weeping.
The Lord has listened to my pleas;
the Lord has accepted my prayer.

All my enemies will be shamed and terrified;
they will flee in utter confusion.

(Psalm 6)

Prayer in Time of Trouble

Plea for God's help

O LORD, my God, I take refuge in You;
keep me safe from all my pursuers and deliver me
lest like a lion they tear me to pieces
and carry me off, with no one to rescue me.

Cry of innocence

O Lord, my God, if I have done this,
if my hands are stained with guilt,
if I have repaid a friend with treachery—
I who spared the lives of those who without cause were my enemies—
then let my foe pursue and overtake me;
let him trample my life into the ground
and leave my honor in the dust.

Appeal to God's judgment

Rise up, O Lord, in Your indignation;
rise against the fury of my enemies.
Rouse Yourself for me,
and fulfill the judgment You have decreed.

Let the peoples assemble in Your presence
as You sit above them enthroned on high.
The Lord is the judge of the nations.

Therefore, pass judgment on me, O Lord, according to my righteousness,
according to my innocence, O Most High.
Put an end to the malice of the wicked
but continue to sustain the righteous,
O God of justice,
You Who search minds and hearts.

(Psalm 7:1-10)

Prayer Extolling the Majesty of God and the Dignity of Man

Man's finite nature and God's infinite majesty

O LORD, our Lord,
how glorious is Your name in all the earth!
You have exalted Your majesty above the heavens.
Out of the mouths of newborn babes and infants
You have brought forth praise
as a bulwark against Your foes,
to silence the enemy and the avenger.

When I look up at Your heavens
that have been formed by Your fingers,

the moon and the stars
  that You set in place,
what is man that You are mindful of him,
  the son of man that You care for him?

Man accorded dignity and power by God

You have made him a little less than the angels
  and crowned him with glory and honor.

You have given him dominion over the works of Your hands
  and placed everything under his feet:
all sheep and oxen
  as well as the beasts of the field,
the birds of the air, the fish of the sea,
  and whatever swims in the paths of the sea.

O Lord, our Lord,
  how glorious is Your name in all the earth!
(Psalm 8)

Prayer to God the Supreme Good

The Lord is my portion

I BLESS the Lord Who offers me counsel;
  even during the night my heart instructs me.
I keep the Lord always before me,
  for with Him at my right hand
  I will never fall.

Therefore, my heart is glad
and my soul rejoices;
my body too is filled with confidence.
For You will not abandon me to the netherworld
or allow Your Holy One to suffer corruption.

Joyous resurrection

You will show me the path to life;
You will fill me with joy in Your presence
and everlasting delights at your right hand.
(Psalm 16:7-11)

Prayer of Christ on the Cross

Lament in suffering

MY God, my God, why have You forsaken Me?
Why have You paid no heed to my call for help,
to My cries of anguish?
O My God, I cry by day, but You do not answer,
by night, but I am afforded no relief.

Yet You are enthroned as the Holy One;
You are the praise of Israel.

Our ancestors placed their trust in You;
 they trusted, and You gave them deliverance.
They cried out to You and were saved,
 they trusted in You and were not put to shame.
But I am a worm and not human,
 scorned by people and despised by my kinsmen.
All who see me jeer at me;
 they sneer in mockery and toss their heads:
"He relied on the Lord;
 let the Lord set Him free.
Let the Lord deliver Him,
 if He loves Him."

Yet You brought Me out of the womb
 and made Me feel secure
 upon My mother's breast.
I was entrusted to Your care at My birth;
 from My mother's womb, You have been My God.
Do not remain aloof from Me,
 for trouble is near
 and no one can help Me.

Joy of the risen Savior

I will proclaim Your name to My family;
 in the midst of the assembly I will praise You:

"You who fear the Lord, praise Him.
All you descendants of Jacob, give Him glory.
Revere Him, all you descendants of Israel.
For He has not scorned or disregarded
the wretched Man in His suffering;
He has not hidden His face from Him
but has heeded His call for help."

I will offer My praise to You in the great assembly;
in the presence of those who fear Him, I will fulfill My vows.
The poor will eat and be filled;
those who seek the Lord will praise Him:
"May your hearts live forever."

(Psalm 22:2-12, 23-27)

Prayer to the Good Shepherd

Constant protector

THE Lord is my shepherd;
there is nothing I shall lack.
He makes me lie down in green pastures;
He leads me to tranquil streams.
He restores my soul,
guiding me in paths of righteousness
so that His name may be glorified.
Even though I wander
through the valley of the shadow of death,

I will fear no evil,
  for You are at my side,
with Your rod and Your staff
  that comfort me.

Considerate host

You spread a table for me
  in the presence of my enemies.
You anoint my head with oil;
  my cup overflows.
Only goodness and kindness will follow me
  all the days of my life,
and I will dwell in the house of the Lord
  forever and ever.

(Psalm 23)

Prayer in Time of Fear

Trust in God

THE Lord is my light and my salvation;
  whom should I fear?
The Lord is the stronghold of my life;
  of whom should I be afraid?

When evildoers close in on me
  to devour my flesh,
it is they, my adversaries and enemies,
  who stumble and fall.

Even if an army encamps against me,
  my heart will not succumb to fear;
even if war breaks out against me,
  I will not have my trust shaken.

Secure refuge

There is only one thing I ask of the Lord,
  just one thing I seek:
to dwell in the house of the Lord
  all the days of my life,
so that I may enjoy the beauty of the Lord
  and gaze on His temple.

For He will hide me in His shelter
  in times of trouble.
He will conceal me under the cover of His tent
  and place me high upon a rock.
Even now my head is raised high
  above my enemies who surround me.
In His tent I will offer sacrifices with joyous
    shouts;
  I will sing and chant praise to the Lord.
(Psalm 27:1-6)

Prayer for God's Mercy

Hope of the penitent

O LORD, do not punish me in Your anger
or chastise me in Your wrath.

For Your arrows have pierced me deeply,
and Your hand has come down upon me.

No portion of my body has been unscathed
as a result of Your anger;
my bones have become weak
as a result of my sins.
My iniquities tower far above my head;
they are a burden too heavy to bear.

Sorrow for sin

I am at the point of exhaustion,
and my grief is with me constantly.
I acknowledge my iniquity,
and I sincerely grieve for my sin.

Numerous and strong are my enemies without cause;
many are those who hate me without good reason.
Those who repay my good deeds with evil
oppose me because I follow a path of righteousness.

Do not abandon me, O Lord;
my God, do not remain far from me.
Come quickly to my aid,
O Lord, my Savior.

(Psalm 37:1-5, 18-23)

Prayer of Longing and Hope

Longing to see God

AS a deer longs for running streams,
so my soul longs for You, O God.
My soul thirsts for God, the living God.
When shall I come to behold the face of God?

My tears have become my food
day and night,
while people taunt me all day long, saying,
"Where is your God?"
As I pour out my soul,
I recall those times
when I journeyed with the multitude
and led them in procession to the house of God,
amid loud cries of joy and thanksgiving
on the part of the crowd keeping festival.

Why are you so disheartened, O my soul?
Why do you sigh within me?
Place your hope in God,
for I will once again praise Him,
my Savior and my God.

Hopeful of God's promises

My soul is disheartened within me;
therefore, I remember You

from the land of Jordan and Hermon,
  from Mount Mizar.
The depths of the sea resound
  in the roar of Your waterfalls;
all Your waves and Your breakers
  sweep over me.
During the day the Lord grants His kindness,
  and at night His praise is with me,
  a prayer to the living God.

I say to God, my Rock,
  "Why have You forgotten me?
Why must I go about in mourning
  while my enemy oppresses me?"
It crushes my bones
  when my foes taunt me,
jeering at me all day long,
  "Where is your God?"

Why are you so disheartened, O my soul?
  Why do you sigh within me?
Place your hope in God;
  for I will once again praise Him,
  my Savior and my God.

(Psalm 42:2-12)

Prayer before Confession

Sincere sorrow for sin

HAVE mercy on me, O God,
in accord with Your kindness;
in Your abundant compassion
wipe away my offenses.
Wash me completely from my guilt,
and cleanse me from my sin.

For I am fully aware of my offense,
and my sin is ever before me.
Against You, You alone, have I sinned;
I have done what is evil in Your sight.

Therefore, You are right in accusing me
and just in passing judgment.
Indeed, I was born in iniquity,
and in sin did my mother conceive me.

But You desire sincerity of heart;
and You endow my innermost being with wisdom.

Create in me a clean heart, O God,
and renew a resolute spirit within me.
Do not cast me out from Your presence
or take away from me Your Holy Spirit.

Restore to me the joy of being saved,
and grant me the strength of a generous spirit.

Praise of God for His mercy

I will teach Your ways to the wicked,
and sinners will return to You.

Deliver me from bloodguilt, O God,
the God of my salvation,
and I will proclaim Your righteousness.
O Lord, open my lips,
and my mouth will proclaim Your praise.

For You take no delight in sacrifice;
if I were to make a burnt offering,
You would refuse to accept it.
My sacrifice, O God, is a broken spirit;
a contrite and humble heart, O God,
You will not spurn.

(Psalm 51:3-8, 12-19)

Prayer to End Wars

Fortify us against the enemy

O GOD, You have turned away from us
and left us defenseless.
Although Your anger was aroused,
now come to our aid.

You shook the earth and split it apart;
repair its cracks, for it continues to shake.
You have inflicted hardships on Your people;
You have given us wine that made us stagger.

But for those who fear You,
You have raised up a banner
to unfurl against the bow.
With Your right hand come to our aid and answer us
so that those You love may be delivered.

Lead us to victory

Who will lead me into the fortified city?
Who will guide me into Edom?
Is it not You, O God, who have rejected us
and no longer go forth with our armies?

Grant us Your help against our enemies,
for any human assistance is worthless.
With God's help we will be victorious,
for He will overwhelm our foes.

(Psalm 60:3-7, 11-14)

Prayer for Ardent Longing for God

Thirst for God

O GOD, You are my God,
for Whom I have been searching earnestly.
My soul yearns for You
and my body thirsts for You,
like the earth when it is parched,
arid and without water.

I have gazed upon You in the sanctuary
so that I may behold Your power and Your glory.
Your kindness is a greater joy than life itself;
thus my lips will speak Your praise.

Union with God

I will bless You all my life;
with uplifted hands I will call on Your name.
My soul will be satisfied as at a banquet
and with rejoicing lips my mouth will praise You.

I think of You while I lie upon my bed,
and I meditate on You during the watches of the night.
For You are my help,
and in the shadow of Your wings I rejoice.
My soul clings tightly to You;
Your right hand holds me fast.

(Psalm 63:2-9)

Prayer for Help against Enemies

Protection from enemies

LISTEN, O God, to my cry of lament;
from the dreaded enemy preserve my life.

Protect me from the council of the wicked,
from the band of those who do evil.

They sharpen their tongues like swords,
and they shoot forth their venomous words
like arrows,
while they attack the innocent from ambush,
shooting suddenly and without fear.

They agree on their evil plan,
and they resolve to lay snares,
saying, "Who will see us?"
They plot evil schemes
and devise shrewd plots;
the thoughts of their hearts are hidden.

God's punishment

However, God will shoot His arrows at them,
and they will suddenly be struck down.
Their own tongues will bring them down,
and all who see them will wag their heads.

Then everyone will be in awe,
as they proclaim God's mighty deeds
and contemplate what He has done.
The righteous will rejoice in the Lord
and take refuge in Him;
all the upright in heart will praise Him.

(Psalm 64)

Prayer of Thanks

Gratitude

IT is fitting to offer praise to You,
  O God, in Zion.
To You our vows must be fulfilled,
  for You answer our prayers.
To You all flesh must come,
  burdened by its sinful deeds.
Too heavy for us are our sins,
  and only You can blot them out.

Blessed is the one whom You choose
  and invite to dwell in Your courts.
We will be filled with the good things of Your house,
  of Your holy temple.

God's bountiful harvest

You care for the earth and water it,
  making it most fertile.
The streams of God are filled with water
  to provide grain for its people.
Thus, You prepare the earth for growth:
  You water its furrows
  and level its ridges;
You soften it with showers
  and bless its yield.

You crown the year with Your bounty,
and Your tracks dispense fertility.
The pastures of the wilderness overflow,
and the hills are covered with rejoicing.
The meadows are clothed with flocks,
and the valleys are decked out with grain;
in their joy they shout and sing together.
(Psalm 65:1-5, 10-14)

Prayer of a Grateful Heart

Thanksgiving in love

I LOVE the Lord because He has heard my voice
and listened to my cry for mercy,
because He has inclined His ear to me
on the day when I called out to Him.

The bonds of death encompassed me;
the snares of the netherworld held me tightly.
I was seized by distress and sorrow.
Then I cried out in the name of the Lord:
"O Lord, I entreat You to preserve my life."

Petition granted

Gracious is the Lord and righteous;
our God is merciful.
The Lord watches over His little ones;
when I was brought low, He saved me.
(Psalm 116:1-6)

Prayer for Spiritual Need

Look to our heavenly Helper

I LIFT up my eyes to You,
to You Who are enthroned in heaven.
Behold, as the eyes of servants
are on the hand of their master,
or as the eyes of a maid
focus on the hand of her mistress,
so our eyes are on the Lord, our God,
as we wait for Him to show us His mercy.

Prayer of pity

Show us Your mercy, O Lord, show us Your mercy,
for we have suffered more than our share of contempt.
We have had to suffer far too long
the insults of the haughty
and the contempt of the arrogant.

(Psalm 123)

Prayer for Home Life

Blessings of a good family

BLESSED are all those who fear the Lord
and walk in His ways.
You will eat the fruit of your labors;
you will enjoy both blessings and prosperity.

Your wife will be like a fruitful vine
within your house;
your sons will be like shoots of an olive tree
around your table.
Such are the blessings that will be bestowed
on the man who fears the Lord.

Prosperity and long life

May the Lord bless you from Zion
all the days of your life.
May you rejoice in the prosperity of Jerusalem
and live to see your children's children.
Peace be upon Israel.

(Psalm 128)

Prayer for Pardon and Peace

Plea to be heard

OUT of the depths I cry to You, O Lord;
O Lord, hear my voice.
Let Your ears be attentive
to my cries of supplication.

God's pardon

If You, O Lord, kept a record of our sins,
O Lord, who could stand upright?
But with You there is forgiveness
so that You may be revered.

Trust in God's mercy

I wait for the Lord in anxious expectation;
  I place my hope in His word.
My soul waits for the Lord
  more than watchmen wait for the dawn.

Hope in the Redemption

More than watchmen wait for the dawn
  let Israel wait for the Lord.
For with the Lord there is kindness,
  as well as plenteous redemption.
He alone will redeem Israel
  from all its sins.

(Psalm 130)

Prayer for Fraternal Charity

Holy unity

HOW wonderful and delightful it is
  for brothers to live together in unity.
It is like fragrant ointment poured on the head,
  running down upon the beard,
running down upon the beard of Aaron,
  and flowing on the collar of his robes.
It is like the dew of Hermon
  falling upon the mountains of Zion.
For there the Lord has bestowed His blessing,
  life forevermore.

(Psalm 133)

Prayer of Praise from All Creation

Let all creation praise God

PRAISE God in His sanctuary;
praise Him in the firmament of His power.
Praise Him for His awesome acts,
praise Him for His immeasurable greatness.

Praise Him with the sound of the trumpet,
praise Him with the harp and lyre.
Praise Him with tambourines and dancing,
praise Him with strings and flutes.
Praise Him with clanging cymbals,
praise Him with crashing cymbals.

Let everything that breathes
offer praise to the Lord.

Alleluia.

(Psalm 150)

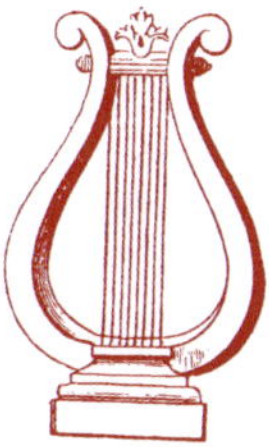

Mary, Mother of our Savior, pray for us.

PRAYERS TO OUR BLESSED MOTHER

(See also pp. 9, 12-14, and 147.)

We Fly to Your Patronage

WE fly to your patronage, O holy Mother of God; despise not our petitions in our necessities, but deliver us always from all dangers, O glorious and blessed Virgin. Amen.

The "Memorare"

REMEMBER, O most gracious Virgin Mary, that never was it known that anyone who fled to your protection, implored your help or sought your intercession was left unaided.

Inspired with this confidence, I fly to you, O Virgin of virgins, my Mother; to you do I come, before you I stand, sinful and sorrowful. O Mother of the Word Incarnate, despise not my petitions, but in your mercy hear and answer me. Amen.

How to Say the Rosary

1. Begin on the crucifix and say the Apostles' Creed.
2. On the 1st bead, say 1 Our Father.
3. On the next 3 beads, say Hail Mary.
4. Next say 1 Glory Be. Then announce and think of the first Mystery and what it means, and say 1 Our Father.
5. Say 10 Hail Marys and 1 Glory Be to the Father.
6. Announce the second Mystery and continue in the same way until each of the five Mysteries of the selected group or decade is said.

The Joyful Mysteries

1. The Angel Gabriel brings the joyful message to Mary. (Lk 1:26-38; Is 7:10-15)
2. Mary visits her cousin Elizabeth. (Lk 1:39-56)
3. Jesus is born in a stable in Bethlehem. (Lk 2:1-14; Mt 1:18-24; Gal 4:1-7)
4. Jesus is offered in the Temple. (Lk 2:22-38)
5. Jesus is found again in the Temple. (Lk 2:42-52)

The Luminous Mysteries

1. Jesus is baptized. (Mt 3:13-17)
2. Jesus manifests Himself at Cana. (Jn 2:1-11)
3. Jesus proclaims the Kingdom of God. (Mk 1:15; Mt 5:1-11)
4. Jesus is transfigured. (Mt 17:1-8; Mk 9:2-8; Lk 9:28-36)
5. Jesus institutes the Eucharist. (Mt 26:26-30; Mk 14:22-26; Lk 22:14-20)

The Sorrowful Mysteries

1. Jesus prays in agony to His Heavenly Father. (Mt 26:36-46)
2. Jesus is scourged. (Mt 27:26)
3. Jesus is crowned with thorns. (Mt 27:27-31)
4. Jesus carries His Cross to Calvary. (Mt 27:32)
5. Jesus dies on the Cross. (Mt 27:33-50; Jn 19:17-30)

The Glorious Mysteries

1. Jesus rises from death. (Mk 16:1-7; Jn 20:1-10)
2. Jesus ascends to Heaven. (Mk 16:19-20; Acts 1:9-11)

3. The Holy Spirit descends upon the Apostles. (Jn 14:15-31; Acts 2:1-11)
4. Mary is taken up to Heaven in body and soul. (Lk 1:41-50; Ps 45; Gn 3:15)
5. Mary is crowned in Heaven. (Rv 12:1; Jdt 13:18-20)

Prayer after the Rosary

O GOD, Whose only-begotten Son, by His Life, Death, and Resurrection, has purchased for us the rewards of eternal life; grant, we ask You, that, meditating upon these Mysteries of the Most Holy Rosary of the Blessed Virgin Mary, we may imitate what they contain and obtain what they promise, through the same Christ our Lord. Amen.

Rosary Novena Prayer

HOLY Virgin Mary, Mother of God and our Mother, accept this Holy Rosary, which I offer you to show my love for you and my firm confidence in your powerful intercession. I offer it as an act of faith in the Mysteries of the Incarnation and the Redemption, as an act of thanksgiving to God for all His love for me and all mankind, as an act of atonement for the sins of the world, especially my own, and as an act of petition to God through your intercession for all the needs of God's people on earth, but especially for this earnest request *(mention your request).*

I beg you, dear Mother of God, present my petition to Jesus, your Son. I know that you want me to seek God's Will in my request. If what I ask for should not be God's Will, pray that I may receive that which will be of greater benefit for my soul. I put all my confidence in you. Amen.

PRAYERS TO ST. JOSEPH
Patron of the Universal Church

Litany of St. Joseph

LORD, have mercy. *Christ, have mercy.*
Lord, have mercy.
Christ, hear us.
Christ, graciously hear us.
God, the Father of Heaven, *have mercy on us.*
God the Son, Redeemer of the world, *have mercy on us.*
God the Holy Spirit, *have mercy on us.*
Holy Trinity, one God, *have mercy on us.*
Holy Mary, *pray for us.* *
St. Joseph,
Renowned offspring of David,
Light of Patriarchs,
Spouse of the Mother of God,
Guardian of the Redeemer,
Chaste guardian of the Virgin,
Foster father of the Son of God,
Diligent protector of Christ,
Servant of Christ,
Minister of salvation,
Head of the Holy Family,
Joseph most just,
Joseph most chaste,
Joseph most prudent,
Joseph most strong,
Joseph most obedient,
Joseph most faithful,
Mirror of patience,
Lover of poverty,
Model of artisans,
Glory of home life,
Guardian of virgins,
Pillar of families,
Support in difficulties,
Solace of the wretched,
Hope of the sick,
Patron of exiles,
Patron of the afflicted,
Patron of the poor,
Patron of the dying,
Terror of demons,
Protector of Holy Church,
Lamb of God, You take away the sins of the world; *spare us, O Lord!*
Lamb of God, You take away the sins of the world; *graciously hear us, O Lord!*

* *Pray for us* is repeated after each invocation.

Lamb of God, You take away the sins of the world; *have mercy on us.*

℣. He made him the lord of His household.
℟. *And prince over all His possessions.*

To You, O Blessed Joseph

TO You, O blessed Joseph,
do we come in our tribulation,
and having implored the help of your most holy spouse,
we confidently invoke your patronage also.
Through that charity that bound you
to the Immaculate Virgin Mother of God
and through the paternal love
with which you embraced the Child Jesus,
we humbly beg you graciously to regard
the inheritance that Jesus Christ has purchased by His Blood,
and with your power and strength to aid us in our necessities.

O most watchful guardian of the Holy Family,
defend the chosen children of Jesus Christ;
O most loving father,
ward off from us every contagion of error and corrupting influence;
O our most mighty protector,
be propitious to us and from heaven assist us
in our struggle with the power of darkness;

and, as once you rescued the Child Jesus from deadly peril,
so now protect God's Holy Church
from the snares of the enemy and from all adversity;
shield, too, each one of us by your constant protection,
so that, supported by your example and your aid,
we may be able to live piously,
to die holily,
and to obtain eternal happiness in heaven. Amen.

Partial indulgence.

Prayer for the Whole Church

O GLORIOUS St. Joseph,
you were chosen by God to be
the foster father of Jesus,
the most pure spouse of Mary, ever Virgin,
and the head of the Holy Family.
You have been chosen by Christ's Vicar
as the heavenly Patron and Protector
of the Church founded by Christ.

Protect the Sovereign Pontiff
and all bishops and priests united with him.

Be the protector of all who labor for souls
amid the trials and tribulations of this life;
and grant that all peoples of the world
may be docile to the Church
without which there is no salvation.

Dear St. Joseph,
accept the offering I make to you.
Be my father, protector, and guide
in the way of salvation.
Obtain for me purity of heart
and a love for the spiritual life.
After your example,
let all my actions be directed
to the greater glory of God,
in union with the Divine Heart of Jesus,
the Immaculate Heart of Mary,
and your own paternal heart.
Finally, pray for me
that I may share in the peace and joy
of your holy death.

Prayer for the Spirit of Work

GLORIOUS St. Joseph,
model of all who pass their life in labor,
obtain for me the grace to work in a spirit of penance

to atone for my many sins;
to work conscientiously,
putting the call of duty above my own inclinations;
to work with gratitude and joy,
considering it an honor to use and develop by my labor
the gifts I have received from God;
to work with order, peace, moderation, and patience,
without ever recoiling before weariness or difficulties.

Help me to work, above all, with purity of intention
and with detachment from self,
having always before my eyes the hour of death
and the accounting that I must render
of time lost, talents wasted, good omitted,
and vain complacency in success,
which is so fatal to the work of God.
All for Jesus,
all for Mary,
all after your example,
O Patriarch Joseph!
This shall be my watchword in life and in death.

Prayer to Know One's Vocation

O GREAT St. Joseph,
you were completely obedient
to the guidance of the Holy Spirit.
Obtain for me the grace to know the state of life
that God in His Providence has chosen for me.
Since my happiness on earth,
and perhaps even my final happiness in heaven,
depends on this choice,
let me not be deceived in making it.

Obtain for me the light to know God's Will,
to carry it out faithfully,
and to choose the vocation
that will lead me to a happy eternity.

Prayer for a Happy Death

O BLESSED Joseph,
you gave forth your last breath
in the loving embrace of Jesus and Mary.
When the seal of death shall close my life,
come with Jesus and Mary to aid me.
Obtain for me this solace for that hour—

to die with their holy arms around me.
Jesus, Mary, and Joseph,
I commend my soul, living and dying,
into your sacred arms.

Invocations to St. Joseph

ST. JOSEPH,
help us to lead an innocent life,
and keep it ever safe under your patronage.

ST. JOSEPH,
foster father of our Lord Jesus Christ,
and true spouse of the Virgin Mary,
pray for us.

JESUS, Mary, and Joseph,
bless us now and in death's agony.

Our Blessed Mother and the Saints are our advocates before God.

PRAYERS TO PATRON SAINTS

Prayer to Our Lady of Perpetual Help

O MOTHER of Perpetual Help, grant that I may ever invoke your powerful name, which is the safeguard of the living and the salvation of the dying. O pure Virgin Mary, let your name be henceforth ever on my lips. Whenever I call on you by name, hasten to help me. When I speak your sacred name or even think of you, what consolation and confidence, what sweetness and emotion fill my soul!

I thank God for having given you so sweet, powerful, and lovely a name for my good. Let my love for you prompt me ever to greet you as Mother of Perpetual Help.

Prayer to St. Jude

Patron of Desperate Cases

O GLORIOUS St. Jude, you were honored to be a cousin as well as a follower of Jesus, and you wrote an Epistle in which you said: "Grow strong in your holy faith through prayer in the Holy Spirit." Obtain for us the grace of being people of faith and people of prayer. Let us be so attached to the three Divine Persons through faith and prayer on earth that we may be united with them in the glory of the Beatific Vision in heaven.

Prayer to St. Anthony of Padua

Patron of All Who Seek Lost Articles

DEAR St. Anthony, you are the patron of the poor and the helper of all who seek lost articles. Help me to find the object I have lost so that I will be able to make better use of the time that I will gain for God's greater honor and glory. Grant your gracious aid to all people who seek what they have lost—especially those who seek to regain God's grace.

Prayer to St. Gerard Majella

Patron of Expectant Mothers

DEAR Redemptorist Saint, model Priest and Religious, compassionate toward suffering mothers, intercede for this expectant mother. Let her not be selfish like those who are willing to put an end to the life they bear within themselves. Instead let her remain ever conscious that she is privileged to be the instrument through whom God brings another life into the world. Encourage her for the good of her child and the glory of the Lord of life.

Prayer to St. Peregrine

Patron of Cancer Patients

DEAR Apostle of Emilia and member of the Order of Mary, you spread the Good News by your word and by your life witnessed to its truth. In union with Jesus cruci-fied, you endured excruciating sufferings so patiently as to be healed miraculously of cancer in the leg. If it is agreeable to God, obtain relief and cure for N. and keep us all from the dread cancer of sin.

Prayer to St. Charles Borromeo

Patron of Catechists

O SAINTLY reformer, animator of spiritual renewal of priests and religious, you organized true seminaries and wrote a standard catechism. Inspire all religious teachers and authors of catechetical books. Move them to love and transmit only that which can form true followers of the Teacher Who was Divine.

Prayer to St. Aloysius

Patron of Youth

DEAR Christian youth, you were a faithful follower of Christ in the Society of Jesus. You steadily strove for perfection while generously serving the plague-stricken. Help our youth today who are faced with a plague of false cults and false gods. Show them how to harness their energies and to use them for their own and others' fulfillment—which will redound to the greater glory of God.

Prayer to St. Thomas Aquinas

Patron of Students

WONDERFUL theologian and Doctor of the Church, you learned more from the Crucifix than from books. Combining both sources, you left us the marvelous *Summa* of theology, broadcasting most glorious enlightenment to all. You always sought for true light and studied for God's honor and glory. Help us all to study our religion as well as all other subjects needed for life, without ambition and pride in imitation of you.

Prayer to St. John Baptist de la Salle

Patron of Educators

WELL-KNOWN Founder of the Congregation of the Brothers of Christian Schools, orthodox and prayerful theologian, you realized the very great value of competent Christian educators. How great your wholesome influence has been! Make your followers continue to be Christlike models for all their students who in turn will edify others.

Prayer to St. Isidore the Farmer

Patron of Farmers

DEAR Isidore, you know how normal it is to cultivate the land for you were employed as a farm laborer for the greater part of your life. Although you received God's help materially through Angels in the field, all farmers are aided spiritually to see the wonders God has strewn on this earth. Encourage all farmers in their labors and help them to feed numerous people.

We follow Jesus' example in our love and concern for one another.

PRAYERS OF PETITION FOR HOLINESS OF LIFE

To Love God Above All

GOD, my Father,
may I love You in all things
and above all things. May I reach the joy
You have prepared for me in heaven.
Nothing is good that is against Your Will,
and all is good that comes from Your hand.
Place in my heart a desire to please You
and fill my mind with thoughts of Your love,
so that I may grow in Your wisdom
and enjoy Your peace.

To Become More Like Jesus

GOD, our Father, You redeemed us
and made us Your children in Christ.
Through Him You have saved us from death
and given us Your Divine life of grace.
By becoming more like Jesus on earth,
may I come to share His glory in heaven.
Give me the peace of Your kingdom,
which this world does not give.
By Your loving care
protect the good You have given me.
Open my eyes to the wonders of Your love
that I may serve You with a willing heart.

The Way to Peace

FATHER of love, hear my prayer.
Help me to know Your Will
and to do it with courage and faith.
Accept my offering of myself—
all my thoughts, words, deeds and sufferings. May my life be spent giving You glory.
Give me the strength to follow Your call,
so that Your truth may live in my heart
and bring peace to me and to those I meet
for I believe in Your love.

To Know the Way to Peace

FATHER of heaven and earth, hear my prayer,
and show me the way to peace.
Guide each effort of my life,
so that my faults and my sins
may not keep me from the peace You promised.
May the new life of grace You give me
through the Eucharist and prayer
make my love for You grow
and keep me in the joy of Your Kingdom.

To Follow Mary's Example

LORD Jesus Christ,
help me to follow the example of Mary,
always ready to do Your will.

At the message of an Angel
she welcomed You, God's Son,
and, filled with the light of Your Spirit,
she became Your temple.
Through her prayers for me
take away my weakness
and make the offering of my life with You
in the Holy Sacrifice of the Mass
pleasing to You and to the Father.
May I rejoice in the gift of Your grace
and be united with You and Mary in glory.

For Faith, Hope, Love

LORD my God,
help me to love You with all my heart
and to love all people as You love them.
May I serve You with my every desire
and show love for others even as You love me.
May my faith continue to grow.
Give me the grace I need for my salvation.
Watch over me,
for all my hope is in You.
Through Your mercy and loving kindness,
through the offering of Jesus in the Mass,
and the prayers of His loving Mother,
grant me Your blessings to lead me
to the treasures of Your heavenly Kingdom.

To Live in God's Presence

GOD, my Father,
You have promised to remain forever
with those who do what is just and right.
Help me to live in Your presence.
The loving plan of Your wisdom
was made known when Jesus, Your Son,
became man like one of us.
I want to obey His commandment of love
and bring Your peace and joy to others.
Keep before me the wisdom and love
You have made known in Your Son.
Help me to be like Him in word and deed.

To Share the Life of Jesus

LOVING Father,
faith in Your word is the way to wisdom.
Help me to think about Your Divine plan
that I may grow in the truth.
Open my eyes to Your deeds,
my ears to the sound of Your call,
so that my every act
may help me share in the life of Jesus.
Give me the grace to live the example
of the love of Jesus,
which I celebrate in the Eucharist
and see in the Gospel.
Form in me the likeness of Your Son
and deepen His life within me.

To Turn from Sin

FATHER, Your love never fails.
Keep me from danger
and provide for all my needs.
Teach me to be thankful for Your gifts.
Confident in Your love,
may I be holy by sharing Your life,
and grant me forgiveness of my sins.
May Your unfailing love
turn me from sin
and keep me on the way that leads to You.
Help me to grow in Christian love.

For Faith in God's Truths

MERCIFUL Lord, hear my prayer.
May I who have received Your gift of faith
share forever in the new life of Christ.
May the continuing work of our Redeemer
bring me eternal joy.
You have freed us from the darkness
of error and sin.
Help me to believe in Your truths faithfully.
Grant that everything I do
be led by the knowledge of Your truth.
May the Eucharist give me Your grace
and bring me to a new life in You.

For the Spirit of Truth

FATHER, God of love,
guide me with Your Holy Spirit
that I may honor You,
not only with my lips,
but also with the life I lead,
and so enter Your Kingdom.
Send me Your Spirit
to teach me Your truth
and guide my actions in Your way of peace.
You are my Guide and Protector.
Grant me the grace to love You more.

For the Life of Grace

ALMIGHTY God,
my hope and my strength,
without You I fall into sin.
Help me to follow Jesus faithfully
and to live according to His Will.
Grant me a lasting respect for You
and keep me always in Your love.
Make me holy in mind and heart
and make me always eager to serve You
with all the love of my heart.
May the Body and Blood of Your Son,
which You give me in the Eucharist,
renew Your life of grace within me
that I may grow in Your love.

For God's Guidance

FATHER in heaven,
you made me Your child
and call me to walk in the light of Christ.
Free me from darkness
and keep me in the light of Your truth.
The light of Jesus
has scattered the darkness of hatred and sin.
Called to that light I ask for Your guidance.
Form my life in Your truth,
my heart in Your love.
Through the Holy Eucharist
give me the power of Your grace
that I may walk in the light of Jesus
and serve Him faithfully.

For the Joy of Forgiveness

HEAVENLY Father,
through the obedience of Jesus,
Your Son and Your Servant,
You raised a fallen world.
Free me from sin
and give me the joy of Your forgiveness.
Let sin never lead me astray.
Make me one with You always,
that my joy may be holy and true.
May Your love make me
what You have called me to be,
Your loving child and faithful servant.

To Follow Christ's Example

LORD Jesus, my Friend,
help me to be like You,
Who loved people and died for our salvation.
Inspire me by Your love,
and guide me by Your example.
Change my selfishness into self-giving;
free me from every evil
and help me to serve You with all my heart.
Keep me from my old and sinful ways
and help me to continue in the new life
of Your grace and love.
May Your Eucharist renew me
and bring me to eternal life.

An Offering of the Eucharist

GOD our Father,
Your light of truth guides us
to the way of Christ.
May I who wish to follow Him
reject what is contrary to His Gospel.
I offer You the Eucharist
to the glory of Your Name.
May it make me pure and holy
and bring me closer to eternal life.
May I never fail to praise You
for the life and salvation You give me
for the Sacrament of the Altar.

For the Peace of Christ

GOD, my Father,
from You I have my being.
Be close to me and hear my prayer.
Look upon me in my moments of need,
for You alone can give me true peace.
May I share in the peace of Christ.
Gifts without measure
flow from Your goodness to bring me peace.
My life is Your gift.
Guide my life's journey,
for only Your love makes me happy.
Keep me strong in Your love
and give me Your peace.

For Forgiveness of Sin

HEAVENLY Father, Creator of all,
may I serve You with all my heart
and know Your forgiveness in my life.
Forgive my sins and give me Your life,
Your grace and Your holiness.
Look upon me in my moments of need,
for You alone can give me true peace.
May I share in the peace of Christ
Who offered His life in the service of all.
Help me with Your kindness.
Make me strong through the Eucharist.
May I put into action the saving mystery
I celebrate in the Mass.

Protect me with Your love
and prepare me for eternal happiness.

To Serve God Well

FATHER of mercy, forgive my failings,
keep me in Your peace
and lead me in the way of salvation.
Give me strength in serving You
as a follower of Christ.
May the Eucharist bring me Your forgiveness and give me freedom to serve You all my life. May it help me to remain faithful
and give me the grace I need in Your service.
May it teach me the way to eternal life.

To Be Cleansed from Sin

JESUS, my Redeemer,
You reward virtue and forgive the sinner.
Grant me Your forgiveness
as I come before You confessing my guilt.
May the power of Holy Mass
wash away my sins, renew my spiritual life,
and bring me to salvation.
May I never misuse Your healing gifts,
but always find in them
a source of life and salvation.
Cleanse me of sin and free me from guilt,
for my sins bring me sorrow
but Your promise of salvation brings me joy.

To Follow the Good Shepherd

MY God and Father,
give me new strength from the courage of Christ,
our Savior and Redeemer.
He is our Good Shepherd.
Let me hear the sound of His voice,
lead my steps in the path He has shown,
that I may receive His help
and enjoy the light of Your presence forever.
Strengthened by the Eucharist,
may I feel its saving power in my daily life
till I reach eternal life with You.
Lead me to join the Saints in heaven.

For Health of Mind and Body

GOD of mercy and love,
protect me from all harm.
Give me health in mind and body
to do Your work on earth.
Pour out Your Spirit upon me,
and grant me the strength of the Eucharist,
this Food from heaven,
that I may more willingly
give my life in Your service.
Work in my life with Your grace
and bring me to the joy You promise.

To Be Faithful in Serving God

FATHER in heaven,
ever-living Source of all that is good,
keep me faithful in serving You.
Help me to drink of Christ's truth,
and fill my heart with His love
so that I may serve You in faith and love
and reach eternal life.
In the Sacrament of the Eucharist
You give me the joy of sharing Your life.
Keep me in Your presence.
Let me never be separated from You
and help me to do Your Will.

To Grow in God's Love

LORD, my God,
increase my eagerness to do Your Will
and help me to know
the saving power of Your love.
My heart desires Your love
and my mind searches for the light
of Your Divine Word.
Give me strength
to grow in my love for Christ, my Savior,
that I may welcome the light of His truth.
Give me the grace to do good
that I may reach the Kingdom of Heaven.

For the Light of Faith

LORD Jesus, Light of the world,
fill me with the light of faith.
May that faith shine in my words and deeds.
Open my heart to receive Your life
that I may be filled with Your glory and peace.
May I share Your life completely
by living as You taught.
Make me faithful to You
that I may bring Your life to others.
Help me to live as God's child
and welcome me into Your Kingdom.

To Share the Eucharist

JESUS, my Savior,
You are my Food from heaven.
By my sharing in this mystery of the Eucharist
teach me to judge wisely the things of earth
and to love the things of heaven.
May my communion with You
teach me to love heaven.
May its promise and hope guide my way.
May it help me in my weakness
and free me from sin.
As I serve You here on earth,
strengthen me with the Bread of heaven.

For the Gift of the Holy Spirit

JESUS, Divine Word of God,
You became Man, born of the Virgin Mary. May I come to share Your Divinity,
for You humbled Yourself
to share our human nature.
As You nourish me
with the Food of life in the Eucharist,
give me also Your Spirit,
so that I may be filled with light
at Your coming to my soul.
Lead me to rejoice in true peace.

For Eternal Life with God

HEAVENLY Father,
in glorifying Jesus
and sending us Your Spirit,
You open the way to eternal life.
May my sharing in this gift
increase my love
and make my faith grow stronger.
Send Your Spirit to cleanse my life
so that the offering of myself to You at Mass
may be pleasing to You.
May my sharing in the Eucharist,
our Bread of Life,
bring me to eternal life.

To Receive God's Spirit

FATHER of light,
from Whom every good gift comes,
send Your Spirit into my life
that I may serve You with a holy heart.
Strengthen me with Your Holy Spirit
and fill me with Your light.
Send the Spirit of Pentecost into my heart
to keep me always in Your love.
Enrich me with Your grace
so that I may praise You always
and reach eternal life.
Fulfill my hope
to see You face to face in heaven.

To Be an Offering with Jesus

LORD Jesus,
may everything I do begin with Your grace,
continue with Your help,
and be done under Your guidance.
May my sharing in the Mass
free me from my sins
and make me worthy of Your healing.
May I grow in Your love and service
and become a pleasing offering to You,
and with You to the Father.
May this mystery I celebrate
help me to reach eternal life with You.

For Growth in Faith, Hope, Love

ALMIGHTY God,
strengthen my faith, hope, and love.
May I do with a loving heart
what You ask of me
and come to share the life You promise.
Give me fidelity and love
to carry out Your commands.
Only with Your help
can I offer You fitting service and praise.
May I live the Faith I profess
and trust Your promise of eternal life.
May the power of Your love
continue its saving work in my life.

For Faith in the Risen Lord

FATHER, in Your love
You have brought me from evil to good
and from misery to happiness.
Through Your blessings
give me the help I need to continue in virtue.
Make my faith strong and my hope sure.
May I never doubt that You will fulfill
the promises You have made.
May I who am redeemed
by the suffering and death of Christ
always rejoice in His Resurrection.
As I honor His glorious Resurrection,
renew Your gift of Divine life within me.

To Be Grateful for God's Gifts

LORD Jesus Christ,
I believe in You as my God and Savior.
Make me more faithful to Your Gospel.
By sharing in the Eucharist often
may I come to live more fully
the life of grace You have given me.
Keep Your love alive in my heart
that I may become worthy of You.
Teach me to value Your gifts
and ever be grateful for them.
Help me to strive for eternal life.

To Live as a Child of God

FATHER in heaven,
when the Spirit came down upon Jesus
at His Baptism in the Jordan,
You revealed Him as Your own beloved Son.
Keep me, Your child,
born of water and the Spirit,
faithful to my calling.
May I who share in Your life
as your child through Baptism
follow in Christ's path of service to people.
Let me become one in His sacrifice
and hear His word with faith.
May I live as Your child,
following the example of Jesus.

For God's Forgiveness

MERCIFUL Father,
protect me in my fight against evil.
May the light of Your truth
give sight to the darkness of my sinful eyes;
bring me the blessing of Your forgiveness
and the gift of Your light.
Bless me, a sinner,
who asks for Your forgiveness.
Pardon my sins
and keep me faithful to Your Commandments for You do not want sinners to die
but to live with the Risen Christ.

To Share Christ's Resurrection

ALMIGHTY God,
You have given the human race Jesus Christ,
Your Son and our Savior,
as a model of humility and love.
He fulfilled Your Will by becoming Man
and gave His life on the Cross.
May His death give me hope
and strengthen my faith.
May His Resurrection give me grace
to continue in His love
and lead me to salvation.
Help me to bear witness to Jesus
by following His example in His suffering,

and make me worthy to share in His Resurrection.

For the Blessings of Holy Mass

LORD Jesus Christ,
guide me with Your unfailing love.
Protect me from what could harm me
and lead me to what will save me.
Help me always, for without You
I shall surely fail and sin.
Bring me closer to You
through prayer and Holy Communion.
May Holy Mass cleanse me from my sins,
bring me pardon and grace
and lead me to the joy of heaven.

To Be a Follower of Jesus

LORD Jesus Christ,
fill my heart with faith and love.
Fill my mind with the light of Your Gospel,
that my thoughts and actions may please You,
and my love be sincere.
Look with love upon me,
the love that You showed us
when You delivered Yourself to evil men
and suffered the agony of the Cross.
Teach me to follow Your example.
May my faith, hope, and love
turn hatred to love, conflict to peace,
and death to eternal life.

To Live a Life of Prayer

LORD Jesus,
help me to understand the meaning
of Your Death and Resurrection.
I call out for Your mercy.
Bring me back to You
and to the life You won for us
by Your Death on the Cross and Resurrection.
Help me to grow in faith and hope,
and deepen my love for You in Holy Communion.
Help me to live a life of prayer
according to Your words in the Gospel,
and seek You, Jesus, my Bread of Life,
in the Holy Eucharist.

For the Wisdom of Christ

JESUS, my Savior,
bring me back to You
and fill my mind with Your wisdom.
May my offering in the Mass,
this Sacrament of Your love,
be pleasing to You and to the Father.
Through this Sacrament
may I rejoice in Your healing power
and enjoy Your saving love in mind and body.
May I who receive this Sacrament
grow in love for the things of heaven.

For a Happy Death

MY heavenly Father,
in Your loving Son, Who rose from the dead,
our hope of resurrection dawned.
The sadness of death gives way
to the bright promise of immortality.
For Your faithful people
life is changed, not ended.
Your Son accepted death for love of You
and for the salvation of my soul.
In His Name I ask for the grace
to persevere to the end in Your love.
Keep me watchful at all times.
Keep me obedient to Your Will till death.
May I leave this world with confidence and peace
and come to share
in the gift of Christ's Resurrection.
May I be free from sin when I die
and rejoice in peace with You forever.
May I gain an eternal dwelling place in heaven.

INDEX OF PRAYER THEMES

(Bold type indicates the main divisions of the book.)

ISBN 978-1-953152-41-1
90000
9 781953 152411